Exploring

Quadra

Island

Heritage Sites

&

Hiking Trails

Jeanette Taylor & Ian Douglas

Photo credits: BCARS = British Columbia Archives & Records Service; MCR = Museum at Campbell River. Images © Ian Douglas, except where otherwise noted.

Printed and bound in Canada

Published by Fernbank Publishing
P.O. Box 368, Quathiaski Cove, B.C. Canada V0P 1N0
250.285.3651   Jtaylor@connected.bc.ca

Cover, page design by Islandsynergy Communications
Editing by Tanya Storr and Bill Mathis; Maps by Rob Simpson

Published with the generous assistance of:

Comox-Strathcona Regional District,
Jim Abram, Area J Director

Quadra Credit Union

Quadra Foods

Spirit of the West Kayaking Adventures

Taku Resort

Walcan Seafood Ltd.

National Library of Canada Cataloguing in Publication Data

Taylor, Jeanette, 1953-
  Exploring Quadra Island

  Includes bibliographical references and index.
  ISBN 0-9688890-0-X

  1. Historic sites--British Columbia--Quadra Island--Guidebooks.
2. Hiking--British Columbia--Quadra Island--Guidebooks. 3. Trails--British Columbia--Quadra Island--Guidebooks. 4. Quadra Island (B.C.)--Guidebooks.
I. Douglas, Ian, 1954- II. Title.
FC3845.Q26A3 2001   971.1'2   C2001-910641-6
F1089.V3T39 2001

Contents

Preface

The authors would like to thank the Quadra Island Conservancy and Stewardship Society, Mitlenatch Field Naturalist Society, Quadra Trails Committee, Quadra Island Mapping Project, and numerous individuals who pitched in to make this project possible.

Special thanks to Stan Beech, David Broadland, Betty Brooks, Annabelle Cameron, Syd Cannings, Maryjane Crawley, Emma Douglas, Christian Gronau, the late Tom Hall, Joy Inglis, Rob James, Judy Johnson, Rolf and Heather Kellerhals, Noel Lax, Dave Leadbitter, Richard Leicester, Don McEachern, the late Grace McPherson, Eileen Mackay, Will Marsh, Steve Mooney, Ian Moul, David and Clair Oppenheim, Sandra Parrish of the Museum at Campbell River, Stan and Lynn Patterson, Terry Phillips, Jocelyn Reekie, Liam Sherin, George Sirk, Sandy Spearing, Hope Spencer, Sue Staniforth, Hilary Stewart, Bob Sutherland, Leona Taylor, Howard Telosky, Jim Thomson, Bob Toelle, Brigid Weiler, Susan Westren, Ruby (Hovell) Wilson, and Annette Yourk.

Hiking Safety

Trails described in this guide range from a pleasant stroll to an all-day adventure. Since coastal weather is extremely variable, hikers should be prepared with adequate footwear, weatherproof clothing, water, snacks, first aid kit, and a good map. Letting someone know where you are going and when you plan to be back is always a good idea. Over time, timber access roads change and trail conditions vary, so it is up to each individual hiker to assess current conditions before setting out. Enjoy!

Introduction

Quadra Island is the largest of an archipelago at the northern end of Georgia Strait, known collectively as the Discovery Islands. Packed into a narrow ocean trough, so close to Vancouver Island and the Mainland that both seem deceptively near, these islands are surrounded by views of massive, snow-covered peaks on either shore. Quadra Island is 41.6 kilometres (26 miles) long and up to 9.6 kilometres (6 miles) wide. Its richly varied geography of mountains, forests, lakes, bays, and harbours provides the framework for the colourful human history and splendid natural history.

Most of the island's population of approximately 3,500 people live on the narrow southern peninsula. The bulbous northern portion, which comprises three-quarters of the land mass, is largely undeveloped and held in timber leases, interspersed with parks and protected areas where diligent community groups have created networks of trails.

This book serves as a guide to 22 heritage sites, hiking trails and canoe/kayak routes on Quadra Island, all of them scenic and some possessing haunting links to the past. Hikes along the rocky bluffs of the Chinese Mountains, with their 60-degree views of the Discovery

The first May Day celebration took place on Quadra Island in 1897. In 1998 there was a weekend of festivities—a reunion for longtime residents and a gathering of former May Queens and May pole dancers. **Exploring Quadra Island** *was initiated by the Centenary Committee of Quadra Recreation Society.*

Hope Spring

ferry to Cortes Island

Heriot Bay Inn

Rebecca Spit Prov. Park

Gowlland Harbour

Bryant's Place

Haskin's Trail

Quathiaski Cove

ferry to Campbell River

Cemetery

Kay Dubois Trail

Cape Mudge Village

Lighthouse

Maple Bank

Tsa·Kwa·Luten

roads
trails
park boundaries

0   1   2   3
½   KM

Map of South Quadra

Islands; paddling through the interconnected Village Bay Lakes system; and bush-whacking to find the remains of an old gold mine, are some of the highlights of north Quadra Island. The south island offers an easily accessible collection of outings of equal beauty and interest. Picnicking at Rebecca Spit Marine Provincial Park, with its graduated vistas of islands and mountains; a visit to the Kwagiulth Museum in the contemporary First Nations village of Cape Mudge; or a ramble along the boulder-strewn beach below Tsa-Kwa-Luten Lodge in search of petroglyphs (ancient carvings in stone), are within a short drive of the Quathiaski Cove ferry dock.

A Brief History of the Island

Tropical Beginnings

It's hard to believe that Quadra once shimmered under an equatorial sun. More than 270 million years ago, Quadra was part of Wrangellia, a volcanic land mass or terrane, situated far out in the Pacific Ocean. As the North American landmass drifted west with the break-up of the supercontinent Pangaea, Wrangellia drifted 10,000 kilometres (6,000 miles) northwards (at an appropriate island speed—about 7 centimetres (3 inches) a year—half as fast as human hair grows). Eventually Wrangellia collided with western North America to form Vancouver Island, Quadra and the other Gulf Islands, and much of the mainland coast of BC.

Where do we find clues to Quadra's ancient past? Stroll along Open Bay's rocky shore and look carefully for coin-sized ram's horns—the sacred symbol of the god Ammon. Ammonites were sea creatures related to the Nautilus, a modern cephalopod that also has a curved gas-filled body chamber. The brown and green volcanic rock (known as

Limestone infolding on Breton Island.
Photographer: Christian Gronau.

the Karmutsen formation) on the north end of Quadra piled up on the sea floor over a five million–year period in the middle Triassic. In *West Coast Fossils: A Guide to Ancient Life of Vancouver Island*, the authors describe how the ammonites that flourished while this submarine lava field was forming ended up as a few thin interbeds of fossil-bearing limestone and shale. This limestone band, lying across Quadra from Open Bay to Granite Bay, has been dissolved by groundwater, leaving it with distinctive landforms called Karst topography. Caves, grikes (narrow openings), and sinkholes are examples of modified limestone features. Many of the island's mineral claims, including the Lucky Jim Gold Mine, lie close to this limestone belt.

Then Came the Ice

In the last two million years or so, there have been several major glaciations across North America. The last of these, known in this region as the Fraser Glaciation, began 25,000-30,000 years ago and ended around 10,000 years ago. By drilling core samples and comparing sea levels, scientists estimate that the maximum depth of the ice sheet in the Georgia Basin was nearly 2 kilometres (1.2 miles).

The bluff at Cape Mudge is made up of glacial deposits. Among these are the Quadra Sands, which were deposited by meltwaters in front of the advancing glaciers. Carbon-dated wood fragments from the Quadra Sands (found on nearby Marina Island) indicate the sands were deposited around 20,000 years ago, close to the peak of the Fraser Glaciation. Much later, as the glaciers were retreating, other deposits were laid down over the Quadra Sand. They include glacial till (a jumbled mixture of sand, silt, clay, and larger particles) which was left with sands and gravels over much of the south end of the island.

Following glaciation the sea level stood much higher on the land than it does today, despite the fact that the sea level was actually lower than today. The reason for this disparity is that the earth's crust had been greatly depressed under the massive weight of the glaciers. The land was so low that the sea washed over the lowlands of southern Quadra Island. Waves and currents reworked the surface of the glacial deposits, leaving the land south of Drew Harbour relatively smooth and flat—a stark contrast to the rugged bedrock on the northern end of the island.

Over the next 2,500 years both the land and sea rose, but the rate of uplift for the land, called glacial rebound, was much faster. Rebecca Spit, a well-known Quadra landmark, is a relatively new addition to the island. Within the last 7,500 years, storms and currents have eroded the bluffs at the south end of the island. Waves and currents moved cobbles and sand up along the east coast, forming Rebecca Spit and Drew Harbour.

Island Seasons

Tree frogs chirping…deer wandering along the road at dusk…a flying squirrel gliding from tree to tree—many animals call Quadra home. Here's a look at life in the forests and marshes of the island, compiled from field notes collected over many years by Quadra residents.

January

On crisp January mornings, Harlequin Ducks are often diving for mussels off Rebecca Spit. In between dives, they converse with a series of bath toy squeaks. Both the striking male and less colourful female leave in May to nest near mountain streams. Rafts of black and white sea ducks—Surf and White-winged Scoters, Barrows and Common Goldeneye, Buffleheads—spend the winter in Drew Harbour along with Common Loons. Smaller Pacific Loons, distinguished by a blacker back than other loons in the winter, are more often found in Gowlland Harbour or off Cape Mudge. Winter Wrens, diminutive brown birds with up-tilted tails, are easy to identify, as they are one of the few birds brightening the cold forest with song in January. This is a time of subtle shades of green, when mosses carpeting the forest floor seem to glow in the dim light. Close to a creek you might also hear another bird warbling. The Canning brothers' description of an American Dipper, "a grey tennis ball of a bird nervously doing knee bends on the polished rock," ensures that once you've seen the only songbird that regularly swims, you'll never forget it. Dippers virtually fly along the bottom of brooks, searching for insect larvae and fish eggs, even in the coldest weather. Amazing to watch,

Winter is a great time for watching Harbour Seals.

10

American Dippers often hide their nest behind a waterfall.

Five species of woodpeckers winter on Quadra: Pileated—the large, redheaded, hard-to-miss woodpecker that drills oblong holes while feeding; the Hairy and diminutive Downy; Red-Breasted Sapsucker; and the Northern Flicker. Sapsuckers drill rows of shallow holes in tree bark, returning to drink sap and eat insects. Sapsuckers also have a distinctive rhythmic pattern when drumming in the spring to attract mates; all our other species give a continuous burst of noise. One of the most unique features of woodpeckers, besides being able to withstand brain battering drumming, is a barbed tongue much longer than their head. Useful for snatching grubs out of tunnels, their tongue retracts into a special cavity running around the skull.

Crossing Discovery Passage you often see flocks of Common Murre, a small black and white seabird that nests on the Scott Islands off the tip of Vancouver Island. Dark-eyed Juncos and Varied Thrush (common name is Winter Robin) are frequent feeder visitors. Typical winter flocks include Chestnut-backed Chickadees, Golden and Ruby-crowned Kinglets, Hutton's Vireo, Red-breasted Nuthatch, and Brown Creeper. The ubiquitous Black-tailed Deer, which feed on Western Redcedar, lichens, Douglas-fir, and many garden shrubs, shed their antlers in December and January.

February

Coltsfoot, one of the first flowers to bloom on the coast, can be found along Hyacinthe Creek. Ravens engage in courtship flights that rival the Snowbirds Air Show, and Pileated Woodpeckers drum on dead trees. Screech Owls can be heard calling at dusk, and Great Horned Owls are nesting. By the end of the month, Great Blue Herons have grown breeding plumes, and their bills have started to turn all yellow.

Red-legged Frogs are the first frogs to start breeding in February. Passing air back and forth over their vocal cords, Red-legged Frogs mostly call underwater. Calls given above the water are heard no more than 10 metres (32 feet) away. Each female lays a grapefruit- to canteloupe-sized egg mass, and algae grow around the eggs, supplying oxygen to the developing embryos. The eggs hatch into tadpoles in April, and by July juvenile frogs hop onto land, although these golden-eyed frogs spend most of their lives close to the pond.

Pacific Tree Frogs begin chorusing in February, and mating reaches a peak in March. Although smaller than Red-legged Frogs, the Pacific Tree Frog is loud (movie sound tracks often use their *riv-et* call). They use a throat

patch as a resonance chamber to make a variety of calls: alarm, warning, territorial, and release calls (*cr-e-e-eeek* rainsong is often heard in winter). Tree frogs lay a lemon-sized egg mass with up to 60 eggs, which hatch into golden-flecked tadpoles. The tiny frogs come out of the water in late June and move throughout the forest. They can be bright green or tan coloured. Because special glands produce a waxy coating that allows their skin to stay moist, the frogs are often found far from water.

Pacific Tree Frogs are hard to locate since they cease calling as you approach.

Quadra is a Bullfrog-free zone. Victoria recorded its first Bullfrog back in 1941 (they were introduced to the Pacific Northwest in the 1930s from eastern North America so they could be raised for their big meaty legs), and ever since this loud and voracious frog has been moving steadily up Vancouver Island. Both the Bullfrog tadpoles and adults are larger than any native frog, and with the female being so prolific, laying up to 20,000 eggs, they quickly overwhelm native frog populations. The practice of collecting tadpoles for nature study seems to be the way Bullfrogs reach new territory. An unconfirmed report noted Bullfrogs in the Campbell River area in 2000—so please keep Quadra Bullfrog free.

February is also peak breeding time for wolves that live on the north end of the island. A wolf pack is an extended family, centred on a breeding pair that produces an annual litter of half a dozen pups. Wolves mature in their second year, but a strong social hierarchy ensures that only the dominant male and female breed.

Bumblebees are the first bees to fly each season. Each colony begins with a single queen that comes out from hibernating among dead leaves, having mated with several males the previous fall. She lays eggs in a mouse burrow and incubates them with her body heat. The first brood is all female workers that take over nectar and pollen gathering while the queen lays more eggs. Bumblebee honey is eaten as fast as it is made, which explains why humans don't harvest it, and only well-fed queens survive the winter.

March

March winds bring soaring Turkey Vultures and Bald Eagles. In January, Bald Eagles start rebuilding their nests; many years there are 50 pairs breeding on Quadra. In the Georgia Basin, Bald Eagles prefer to nest in veteran Douglas-firs, but they will use Sitka Spruce, Grand Fir, Cottonwoods and Red Alder in a pinch. A concern about the availability of habitat for the Georgia Basin population has spurred an effort to catalogue and mark nest trees; 450 trees have been noted to date.

Bald Eagles like to be high up—the nest is usually just below the tree top, and partially shaded. Strong branches provide support, as nests may weigh as much as a small car. The eagles pluck branches to give them a clear view and convenient landing space. Active nests can be as close as 1 kilometre (0.6 mile) apart, and both the male and female participate in nest building. Female eagles are up to a third larger than males, with a stockier profile. When both eagles are in the nest, they perch so they have a combined 360-degree view.

Many people have seen the tumbling courtship flights that occur when the male dive bombs the female in midair. She rolls over to meet him and they lock talons, breaking out of the embrace at the last possible moment. Mating occurs on a branch near the nest, not in midair as commonly believed. When she is in the mood, the mating female screams at the male, and when he returns with an offering of nest material, she hops out on a branch and stretches forward. The male hops on her back and mates, wrapping his talons around the female's wings and flapping his wings to maintain balance. The male calls, and after he hops off, the female responds with a screech. Two eggs are laid, usually four days apart, by March 25.

The male eagle brings food to the female during the week she is getting

Bald Eagles don't get their distinctive white head until they are four to five years old.

ready to lay eggs. Dead sea mammals, fish, gulls, and Brant Geese are common items. Once the second egg is laid, the male will relieve the female for a few hours at midday as she goes for food.

The eggs typically hatch by April 30, and the new eaglets, known as eyas, open their eyes after the first week. By three weeks eaglets weigh nearly 2 kilograms (4.4 pounds) and stand 30 centimetres (1 foot) tall. The eaglets can stand up, are feathered and able to tear up their own food and feed themselves at five weeks.

By nine weeks, the young birds' feathers are still developing and not firmly attached to their wing bones. Once the shafts of the feathers are attached to the bone, the bird is ready for vigorous flight. All told, it is about 20 weeks from when the mating pair return to nest until the young fledge; the young won't be on their own for another 10 weeks. By the fourth year, the iris of the Bald Eagle eye turns from brown to yellow. Eagles mate in their fifth or sixth year.

If you are very quiet, you can sometimes watch Bald Eagles bathing in small ponds. They will often perch on a half-submerged log out in the water, since they are vulnerable to predators until their feathers dry. The other time you find wet eagles is when they go after large fish in the ocean. If the fish is too heavy (they can only lift about 2 kilograms or 4 pounds), the eagle has to swim to shore and dry off before it can fly. Vancouver Island naturalists once saw a Sea Lion surface and gulp down a Bald Eagle just after it snagged a salmon.

Robins are on the first of three nests when the first Violet-green Swallows arrive. Noisy flocks of Pine Siskins are busy feeding on Western Hemlock cones, and many people are mistaking the soft call of Band-tailed Pigeons for some kind of owl. The first butterflies to appear on Quadra are the Pacific Orangetip and the Mourning Cloak. In late March, the first tropical migrant to arrive is the Yellow-rumped Warbler.

Some locals refer to the Skunk Cabbage as a swamp lily.

About this time, Northern Stellar Sea Lions and California Sea Lions (adult males have a crested forehead) are feeding on herring by the Breton Islands and over at Deepwater Bay. Skunk Cabbage, also known as swamp lantern, brightens up the drab wetlands with a yellow blaze of colour. While this plant has been maligned for its pungent odour, the broad, soft leaves made an excellent food wrap in traditional First Nations culture. Bees harvest pollen from pussywillows and rusty Red Alder catkins. Blue-eyed Mary is blooming, and if you have a truffle hound, Oregon Truffles can be found in the forest. Rough-skinned Newts migrate to ponds to engage in a mating frenzy from late February to the end of March. Hopeful males remain in the pond till July. The bright orange belly warns predators that newt skin is toxic, but local Garter Snakes have built up immunity. Oblong grape-fruit-sized egg masses found in permanent ponds belong to Northwestern Salamanders.

April

The zip of hummingbirds heralds Salmonberry and Red-flowering Currant blossom time. Male Rufous Hummingbirds appear in mid-March through April, and females arrive a few weeks later. The male Rufous perform a series of J-shaped dive displays that progress in a circle, while the Anna's, which also appear on Quadra, tend to repeat a steep J-shaped dive ending in an explosive buzz/ squeak.

Great Blue Herons nest in small colonies, with females laying four to five eggs in early April. Both parents share incubation and feeding duties when the young are born at the beginning of May. Bald Eagles are a constant threat, as they will take both chicks and adults. Heron parents are very busy from the second half of June until the chicks leave for good around the first week of July. Once they leave the nest, the chicks are on their own, so this is when they may show up at backyard fishponds. Chicks are gray blue with no white on the head or black shoulder patches. Herons feed by following the tide out to catch small fish stranded in pools, so when the tides are minimal in the fall young birds have a tough time finding enough to eat.

By mid-April, Barn Swallows are looking for nest sites, and out in the wooded areas a sound like a distant engine starting indicates a male Ruffed Grouse is ready for love. Pelagic Cormorants and Pigeon Guillemots are getting ready to breed on the Copper Bluffs. Golden-crowned and White-crowned Sparrows are migrating through. Watch for other warbler species such as Orange-crowned and Wilson's that arrive by the end of April. Wood Ducks and Hooded Mergansers are nesting in tree cavities by small ponds.

New leaves cover bare branches with a soft green mantle, and Sea Blush is blooming on rock bluffs. Fawn and Chocolate Lilies are out at Rebecca Spit, and the Fairyslipper Orchid and Western Coralroot are found in deep shade under conifers. Morels and False

Huckleberries were a favourite food for the First Nations.

17

Morels are growing in the forest; if you are unsure of the difference, beware. Monomethyhydrazine—a component of rocket fuel—is given off when False Morels are cooked, and these fumes can be toxic. Domestic honeybees, which were introduced to North America from Europe, are collecting nectar from maples for the first big honey event of the year.

Native plants like the White Fawn Lily are becoming rare.

May

May is the month of bird song. Birds are nesting, and the southern migrants are flying through. Blue Grouse are making booming noises at Bold Point and Nugedzi Lake. Elusive woodland birds singing constantly in second-growth forest are usually Solitary and Warbling Vireos. If you are walking in the woods and it sounds like someone is trying to attract your attention with a "whit" sound, the culprit is a Swainson's Thrush, whose common name is the Salmonberry Bird. The warblers you hear singing are Townsends, Wilsons, and MacGillivrays.

Garter Snakes are sunning themselves on rocks, and the flying ants provide a feast for the Cutthroat in Village Bay Lake. Violet-green Swallows and the second brood of robins are nesting.

Both the Common Camas and Meadow Death-camas are in flower. This is the time of year when the First Nations worked family plots of camas, marking or removing the poisonous white Meadow Death-camas. The blue Common Camas was a staple in the diet of some First Nations groups; baked in steam pits, the bulbs provided a rich, starchy food.

Rusty Saxifrage is blooming on hills, and Western

Trillium is flowering in the forest. Bitter Cherry, Saskatoon, and Red-flowering Currant are major honey producers. Pacific Crabapple blooms in May and June. Broadleaf Starflower, Thimbleberry, Dull Oregon-grape, Vanilla Leaf, Bleeding Heart, and Miner's Lettuce are blooming. Mountain Ash, Salal, Nootka Rose, and Alumroot are also blooming. First Swallowtails, Anglewings, Tortoiseshells, and Cabbage butterflies are making a colourful display. Schools of squid can be seen around the Heriot Bay dock.

June

In early June fawns, usually twins, are born. They are often left in a secluded place by the doe while she goes off to feed on willow, Douglas Maple, and Salal. Nighthawk booming—noise made by wind passing through their primary feathers as they dive—is heard at dusk. Swainson's Thrushes and Chickadees are nesting. A robin-sized canary, better known as the Western Tanager, and Cedar Waxwings arrive. Male hummers are displaying, but by the end of June they move to higher elevations to follow emerging vegetation, leaving the females to raise the young. Quadra's only lizard, the Northern Alligator Lizard, is found on south-facing rocky bluffs.

Bark from Dull Oregon-Grape was used by First Nations to make a yellow dye for baskets.

19

Early June brings Oceanspray, Clover, Twinflower, Fox-glove, the first Huckleberry (they last from June until November), and the first Wild Strawberry. Yarrow is blooming on bluffs, and Nodding Onion is up at Rebecca Spit. At South Chinese Mountains, Twinflower and Blue-bells are blossoming. Labrador Tea and Bog Laurel are flowering in marshy areas. The third week of June until the third week of July is the major honey event of the year when the Himalayan Blackberry buzz with bees. Tiger Lily and Gumweed are blooming.

July

Sandy collars of eggs from the Moon Snail are found on beaches in July; this is a great time to hang over the edge of docks to watch starfish and anemones. Harbour Seals are pupping on the Breton Islands and out on the booms in Gowlland Harbour. Band-tailed Pigeons, Cedar Waxwings, Flickers and Hairy Woodpeckers feast on Elderberries. Mating success for male Cedar Waxwings depends on the redness of their wing tips, which is related to the amount of pigment they ingest in berries. Both the Black-headed and Evening Grosbeaks are singing and feasting on Saskatoon berries. During this time male Harlequin Ducks are in eclipse plumage and can't fly. If it

is a good cone year, flocks of Red Crossbills are around. Indian-pipe, a white and waxy plant that turns black if you pick it, grows close to Douglas-fir on Rebecca Spit. North-

Western Toads make a twittering alarm call, urinate profusely, or secrete a mild poison if grabbed.

western Salamanders, Clouded Salamanders, Ensatinas, Rough-skinned Newts and Western Toads can be found in moist areas under logs.

Dragonflies are mating, while Pacific Damp-wood Termites are flying by the end of the month. Sockeye enter the Village Bay Lake system in July, but hold in Main Lake until October, then make the final trip into Shadow Brook to spawn.

August

The aromatic smell of the forest is a good indicator that this is fire season. The last major fire swept the island in 1925, but every year the volunteer fire department is called out to deal with small blazes. In 1998 a Gray Whale spent the summer in Gowlland Harbour; the next year a mother and calf spent three months feeding amongst the islands. At this time of year, young Bald Eagles are practicing their flying skills around the nest tree. Dozens of Nighthawks are flying at dusk, and the first blip of shorebird migration starts with returns from the breeding areas in the far north: Surfbirds, Turnstones, and Rock and Pectoral Sandpipers. Off north Quadra you can occasionally glimpse Bonaparte's Gulls, Long-tailed and Parasitic Jaegers, as well as Fork-tailed Storm Petrels. Baby Towhees appear about this time. Yarrow, Fireweed, and Douglas Aster are blooming. Campers close to shore wonder if they are hearing gunshots in the night, only to find seals slapping the water with their flippers are the real culprits.

September

September often has the best weather of the year, with warm days and cool nights. Field crickets reach a peak in song, while tropical birds (warblers,vireos, tanagers) begin heading south. Before they leave, they are often seen in mixed foraging flocks along with kinglets and chickadees. Turkey Vultures are also getting ready to head south. In his book *Vultures: Nature's Ghastly Gourmet*, Wayne Grady describes vultures as the bottom feeders of the bird world. "Vultures are our opposites: we smell rotten meat so that we can avoid it; they smell rotten meat so they can find it."

A predominately black bird with a wingspan of nearly 2 metres (6 feet) and red featherless head and neck, a Turkey Vulture soars on dihedral wings. The birds mate for life and although no nest is built, the eggs are elliptical so they will roll in a circle rather than off a cliff edge. Both parents incubate the eggs for 28-41 days before white and downy chicks are born. The most amazing thing about

Fast-swimming Dall's Porpoise (above) and Harbour Porpoise are occasionally seen off Quadra's shores.

vultures is their ability to feed on carrion and survive. Grady explains how this is possible: "The acid in a vulture's digestive track is so strong that botulism and cholera bacteria that would wipe out whole villages pass through vultures like milk through a baby, and studies of vulture excrement show that they actually help control serious outbreaks of anthrax in cattle and swine when they eat infected carcasses; their stomachs destroy the bacteria that cause the diseases."

The beautiful but deadly Fly Agaric Mushroom.

This is the only month that Bald Eagles are hard to find, as the young and adults leave their breeding territories in search of early salmon runs. Some are believed to fly as far as Alaska. Pileated Woodpeckers make pests of themselves pecking holes in apples and pears. Red-necked Phalaropes (common name is the Coho Bird) can be seen from the ferry. Transient Orcas were once seen attacking Pacific White-sided Dolphins and Harbour Seals near the Breton Islands.

September is the peak of Chanterelle and Bolete mushrooms. Fungi form a remarkable partnership with trees. Fungal mats of fine hairs (called mycelium) increase the trees' ability to take up water and trace minerals. In trade, trees give the fungus sugars produced by the leaves. Researchers have found fungi have up to 47 different mycorrhizal associations with Douglas-fir.

Bees seek out Pearly Everlasting, one of the last plants to produce pollen.

October

The maples turn in October, and Snow Geese, Sandhill Cranes, and Canada Geese are on their way south. Sea ducks are back in force: Scoters, Goldeneye, and Common Murre. Commuters on the Quadra ferry may not realize what a birding bonanza Discovery Passage can be at this time of year. A keen birder might pick up a sighting of a Cassin's or Rhino Auklet. Female Harlequins have returned from nesting in the interior, and Marbled Murrelets, called "kiss my ass birds" by fishermen because of the way they duck under to feed, are also off Rebecca Spit. Western Sandpipers, as well as Golden-crowned and White-crowned Sparrows, are migrating through.

Moon and Lions-mane Jellyfish are often stranded at Rebecca Spit after a high tide. Moon Jellyfish polyps overwinter in the shallows and then separate into dozens of free swimming young in the spring. The medusa feed through the summer by trapping small creatures called Copepods in the mucus that coats their bell, then microscopic hairs move the trapped plankton to the underside of the bell and into the mouth. Moon Jellyfish have a very mild sting, but Lions-mane Jellyfish can cause a nasty rash, even after they die on the beach.

November

November is usually the month of rain, as the first of many southeasters hit the island. The jet stream has shifted into the winter pattern, and we experience a new weather system every three or four days. All summer long, fallen trees have stored much-needed moisture for the plants; there is a noticeable change as moss and leaf litter on the forest floor sponge up the extra water. With increased rainfall, Chum and Coho Salmon are able to make their way up creeks to spawn. The abundant runs of salmon that once spawned in every creek and stream on the island were a key staple in the First Nations people's diet. One longtime resident recalled runs of Chum, Coho and Pink spawning in impressive numbers in a small creek in north Gowlland Harbour. Habitat destruction, commercial fishing, and climate change have reduced the overall numbers of fish returning toour streams.

Otters, ravens, and eagles gather to feed on the spawning salmon. Researchers have found that when animals drag the decaying salmon carcasses into the bush, trees along the salmon streams benefit from the increased nitrogen. The easiest place to watch Chum spawning is Granite Bay Creek.

Black-tailed Deer are in rut, and trees bear scars where the stags have scraped their antlers. Deer sometimes munch rockweed on the shore at this time. Trumpeters are flying overhead. During heavy winters, Northern Shrikes and Snowy Owls may appear. If we haven't had a hard frost by now, you can still find Pine Mushrooms.

December

We are nearing the shortest day of the year, and Northern Flying Squirrels looking for shelter sometimes end up in attics. Flying squirrels are fairly common, but they are rarely seen since they are active at night. They can glide more than 80 metres (266 feet) by extending a fold of skin that runs from the wrist along the side of the body to the ankle. They have a flattened tail and weigh less than other tree squirrels. Gliding at an angle of 30 to 40 degrees, they can manoeuvre around tree limbs and other obstacles, even make 90-degree turns. Like any good pilot, they pull up sharply to check their speed at the end of a glide. Flying squirrels eat arboreal lichens during the winter when it is too cold and wet for mushrooms.

Along the stormy shore, Glaucous-winged Gulls and both Pelagic and Double-crested Cormorants are searching for food. Long-tailed Ducks are often found diving at the very end of Rebecca Spit. Western Grebes raft up in large groups between Rebecca Spit and Read Island. Steller's Jays, Dark-eyed Juncos, Fox Sparrows, Rufous-sided Towhees, Varied Thrush, and Golden-crowned Kinglets are frequent feeder visitors.

Generations of Island Life

A complex knowledge of the racing tides that surround Quadra Island was essential for the First Nations people of ancient times. The ghosts of drowned men and women were said to haunt the rocky shores of Seymour Narrows, where a sea monster occasionally surfaced in a boiling mass of whirlpools. And the constricted passage to the north, separating Quadra Island from its close neighbours, Sonora and Maurelle Islands, was no better. Navigating the whirlpools and a reversing falls in Okisollo Channel during the wrong tide remains a challenge for even the most experienced paddler.

The attraction to such a place was its abundance. All five species of salmon could be harvested in Discovery Passage at different times of the year, in impressive numbers. "Nature has made a bountiful provision for these people," wrote James Douglas of the Hudson's Bay Company, in 1840, "they have only to cast their nets into the waters and withdraw them full, as the strait appeared after sunset literally to swarm with fish." From the forests the Native people harvested cedar trees for housing and canoes, took game with bows and arrows, and picked huckleberries and salmonberries to dry for winter use.

At the major clam beds, on the gravelly beaches at Open Bay, Village Bay, Waiatt Bay, Heriot Bay, Kanish Bay,

A heritage sites tour with Spirit of the West Adventures, kayak guides and outfitters. Jeanette Taylor (centre) describes the life of the First Nations people who once used Shell Island, in Granite Bay, as a defensive village site.

Granite Bay, and Gowlland Harbour, they built their principal villages. The depth of the shell middens (refuse piles) at these places bespeak thousands of years of human occupation.[1] Orchard Bay, on the north end of the island, with its 3-metre (10-foot) high bank of shells, is the largest archaeological site on the island. Massive post-and-beam houses, large enough for 20 or more people, were tightly arranged along this shore. Canoes, shaded by mats, sat helter-skelter above the tide line. Families filleted fish on this beach and relaxed in the sun on wooden settees. Highly formalized speeches were exchanged here to negotiate marriage contracts at potlatches, multi-tribe gatherings marking pivotal life events.

At such potlatches, the host clan displayed their hereditary rights in masked dances depicting the beginning of time when magic ancestors transformed from animal to human form, claiming this land and its resources.

The people of the whale clan at Queqakyulis,[2] meaning "whales between the two," sent young men into the harbour in a buoyant representation of a whale controlled by hidden tow lines. As the whale bobbed up and down in the place now called Gowlland Harbour, it spouted feathers.[3] Another family claimed a place called Xaxe, near Cape Mudge, where "a man dropped down from above wearing a swaihwe costume."[4] They possessed the right to the dance of a bug-eyed creature with a great fringe of feathers and jangling, scallop shell rattles.

According to oral history and the journals of eighteenth century European explorers, the people living in this region more than 200 years ago were a Coast Salish tribe, the Island Comox. This large group once consisted of about 10 individual tribes, possessing villages and food gathering sites ranging from Kelsey Bay to just north of Comox. The five top-ranking tribes, who belonged to "the whale house," may have wintered together on the site of the current We-Wai-Kai village at Cape Mudge. In spring, the various clans moved to their fishing, hunting, and berrying grounds.

Such a group was settled at a large village high atop the bluffs at Cape Mudge (current location of Tsa-Kwa-Luten Lodge) in the summer of 1792. From this vantage point, the First Nations people watched as two ships hove into sight, their sails billowing in a westerly breeze. The arrival of these strangers was no surprise to the First Nations people, who must have been aware of the European ships at anchor in Desolation Sound for several weeks prior. As the ships slowly proceeded up the passage, the Native people painted their faces and daubed their hair with eagle down, a gesture of peace and welcome. They were eager for trade, unaware of the insidious cost in loss of life and culture that would ensue.

Captain George Vancouver and the botanist/physician aboard his ship, Archibald Menzies, wrote detailed accounts of their visit to Cape Mudge on July 13, 1792. The day ashore was a welcome relief after many weeks of the "desolate" landscape of their exploration base at Desolation Sound. They had shared this anchorage with Spanish explorers, Galiano and Valdes, who were also meticulously mapping the entire Pacific Northwest coast in search of the fabled Northwest Passage. From Desolation Sound, the Spanish headed north along the mainland coast while the British veered to the northeast, following the Vancouver Island shore. After leaving Cape Mudge, the British continued their

Chief Billy Assu of the We-Wai-Kai Band wearing the marks of his rank, a woven Chilkat blanket, neck ring, and dance headpiece. Photographer: Henry Twidle. **MCR 9105, Dalton Collection.**

laborious mapping, exploring every bay and inlet by small boat. They failed, however, to spot the narrow passage separating the islands of Quadra, Maurelle, and Sonora. As a result these islands were shown as one, under the name Valdez, on the first official charts.

Sometime after the arrival of European explorers, the Island Comox people were all but wiped out. There are scant records of their demise, which may have been the result of a combination of European diseases (for which the Native people had no resistance) and intermittent decades of alternating warfare and intermarriage with a northern group, the Lekwiltok. By the 1860s, the Lekwiltok were in control of Johnstone Strait and Discovery Passage. The few remaining Island Comox families had relocated to

Comox Harbour, their numbers having dropped from many hundred to a few families. As the population shifted, the We-Wai-Kai tribe of the Lekwiltok came to be the dominant group at Cape Mudge.

When the first Euro-Canadian settlers arrived in the early 1880s, the Lekwiltok people, like their Island Comox predecessors, were suffering the ravages of successive waves of newly introduced diseases. Their combined numbers may have been as high as 4,002 people in the 1840s,[5] but by 1881 there were only 381 people left. Most of their non-Native contemporaries passively forecast the pending extinction of the First Nations.

Billy Assu, a chief of a Lekwiltok group, the We-Wai-Kai of Cape Mudge, recalled the arrival of four white men, the first to consider Quadra Island for industry and settlement. The men were treated as guests and supplied with berries and fish, but this hospitality was not an open invitation to settle on the island. In an 1882 newspaper,

The Yeatman family outside their newly completed log home, off Smith Road, circa 1896. The Yeatmans, with their young family, swelled the ranks of the new log school. **MCR 4251, Yeatman Collection.**

Within a few years the Yeatman family's home, was nearly engulfed in hops, grown for bread, and brewing yeast. Pioneers were quick to cover over the log walls of their rustic homes with milled lumber or vines; there was no pride attached to living in a log cabin. Photographer: John Hood. **MCR 4255, Yeatman Collection.**

timber cruisers reported "a jealous feeling among the Lekwiltoks against the possession by white men of land on the island." The Native people were said to be pulling up the surveyors' stakes and falsifying marker trees. This protest proved ineffectual. Loggers and settlers, sanctioned by the government, were not to be stopped. Within two years, 14 properties, encompassing 1,305 hectares (3,263 acres), had been claimed as homesteads and timber leases on Quadra Island.

The government of the day encouraged settlement through a "pre-emption" scheme, providing 64-hectare (160-acre) tracts at $1 per acre. Homesteaders were further required to invest $2.50 per acre in "improvements," which included the value of log homes, outbuildings, clearing, ditching, and fencing.

Clearing the massive stands of Douglas-firs and cedars was a daunting task, so most settlers chose to drain bogs and swamps, digging trenches around and through the rich black soil. According to an early account, a bachelor from Missouri named Charles Dallas was the first non-Native to take up permanent residence on the island, establishing a ranch at Heriot Bay in 1885.[6] He was likely drawn by an intense settlement campaign in 1885, touting the island as a suitable choice for settlement:

The land on Valdez Island is swamp and marsh with fine alder patches. Sufficient land is known to locate about fifteen families. There is a stretch of prairie of about 100 acres without a stick of timber on it, covered with a luxuriant growth of grass. There are also other patches of similar land of smaller extent.

The majority of those who followed Dallas were also bachelors, a free-thinking independent class of men determined to make a place of their own, unfettered by the outside world. They represented a wide variety of ethnic, social, and economic means—from class-conscious English gents to Scandinavian peasants and no-nonsense Scots. Despite the seeming generosity of the pre-emption scheme, many settlers were unable to "prove up" their titles for a decade or more. In truth, the land was best suited to growing trees, though the glowing settlement propaganda described Quadra Island as a poor man's paradise: "The beautiful brown loam [is] well adapted for raising good crops. The resources of the island are stock raising and vegetables. The cattle and hogs roam at large on the fine pasture lands and become fat and good for market." But in fact, those who achieved some measure of success earned their living from a combination of fishing, logging, and subsistence farming.

Boat traffic remained the chief means of transport throughout the settlement era. Four distinct communities developed around safe anchorages in Quathiaski Cove, Heriot Bay, Bold Point, and Granite Bay. By 1910, Heriot

Bay and Quathiaski Cove had the largest communities in the surrounding district, each boasting a population of about 100. A hotel, store, sawmill, and government wharf were opened at Heriot Bay in the 1890s. In Quathiaski Cove a salmon cannery, opened in 1904, was a major employer, along with a sawmill, store, post office, church, and the county courthouse and jail. The few settlers living at what is now Campbell River had to row across to Quathiaski Cove to get their mail and supplies. Granite Bay and Gowlland Harbour both had large logging camps and mines, while Bold Point, across from Read Island, had ranches, a hotel, and a store catering to logging camps.

When it was discovered in the 1870s that Valdez Island was in fact three islands, they came to be known as the Valdez group. In 1903, new names were assigned. The largest became Quadra Island; the other two became Sonora and Maurelle. But for most Valdez Islanders the old name remained firmly fixed in the local vernacular. It wasn't until the 1930s that the new name, Quadra Island, gradually came into use.

The CPR boat, **Princess Beatrice,** *at the dock in Quathiaski Cove. Boat Day was a grand social occasion, when everyone gathered to collect their mail and supplies, and to share the latest news.* **MCR 20126 - 5, McAllister Collection.**

Throughout the settlement era, the We-Wai-Kai people took increasingly independent roles within the new economy developing in their midst, particularly in the fishing industry. First Nations men and women fished by hand and filled salmon cans at the Quathiaski Canning Company. They also formed their own company to log portions of their reserves.

With the technological advances of World War I, cars and trucks gradually superceded boats, and Campbell River gradually took precedence. A major forest fire on Quadra Island in 1925 that wiped out 20,000 hectares (50,000 acres) of merchantable timber and 11 farms hastened the switch. "The many tourists in Campbell River," wrote a newspaper of the day, "witnessed an awe-inspiring sight as miles of flames swept down to the water's edge." Quadra Island then became an isolated backwater, with a declining population, for decades.

Quathiaski Canning Company was a major employer for the region until it was destroyed by fire in 1941. Photo taken c.1914 **MCR 6715.**

Those who remained were a self-reliant lot. The Beech family lengthened an old Model T Ford, converting it into a dual purpose car and tractor with two transmissions, one for bull low and one for speed. The tractor tires, which could be exchanged for road tires, were made from bed frames. Ruby Hovel (later Wilson) and her friends found creative ways to incorporate current fashions into their rural lives. When they left their shift at the cannery, Ruby and her friends hiked up the dirt road to the community dance with their pointy, high heel shoes tucked into their boyfriends' back pockets. These young people could have hailed the local taxi driver, Mrs. Boond, daughter of a British aristocrat, but her fares were pricey and she was a bit of an oddity. Maria Carlotta Boond walked the streets talking to her long-dead mother and shoplifted her groceries at the cannery store. The wary store manager accepted the practise, totting up her "purchases" and adding them to her monthly account, which she usually paid promptly.

The cannery was razed by fire in the summer of 1941 and not replaced, further eroding the island's economy. The first hint of growth and change came when hydro electricity was cabled across the channel from Campbell River in 1951, but it was the inaugural run of the first car ferry in 1960 that brought dramatic change. Islanders could now readily cross over to "the river" to shop, and tourists could motor along the island's dirt roads to camp at the new provincial park at Rebecca Spit or take the twisting road to the island's first resort at April Point. The ferry also brought a new generation of settlers, drop-outs from mainstream society heading "back to the land." These long-haired newcomers upset the social balance of the once isolated community, where there came to be two warring factions, both entrenched in their diverging values. Their one tie, a quality they shared with the First Nations people and the early settlers, was a stubborn self will. Although a kind of truce was eventually established, the two factions still emerge over logging and development issues.

Quadra Island now has a permanent population of approximately 3,500 people, with an economy revolving around service industry businesses, woodlots, sports and commercial fishing, fish farms, tourism, and off-island employment in Campbell River or seasonal jobs elsewhere in silviculture and logging. Walcan Seafood, the largest employer on the island, sends seafood products around the world. Children attend school on Quadra up to grade six, then they join commuters to Campbell River to attend middle school, high school, and college.

The island has two commercial centres, at Heriot Bay and Quathiaski Cove, where there are grocery stores, gift shops, hotels and pubs (with restaurants), post offices, and liquor stores. The Quathiaski Cove shopping area, just uphill from the ferry dock, includes The Landing Pub, Quadra Foods grocery store, a tourist bureau, Quadra Credit Union, a drugstore, a colourful Saturday market, and a gas station at the corner of Harper and Heriot Bay Roads. Heriot Bay also boasts a shopping centre, with a craft shop, grocery store, and art gallery. The venerable Heriot Bay Inn, in business for over a century, offers hotel accommodation, a restaurant, pub, and pads for recreational vehicles. Several up-scale resorts dot the island, including Taku Resort, Tsa-Kwa-Luten Lodge and April Point Lodge, along with a number of bed-and-breakfast operations.

Visitors may want to pick up a comprehensive road map of the island, available at most retail outlets, before heading off on their explorations.

Place Names: *Quadra Island* was named in 1903 to honour the eighteenth-century Spanish explorer, Juan Francisco de la Bodega y Quadra. *Okisollo* (or Ooks-so-lah) translates in Lekwala (Lekwiltok language) to

36

"passageway" (George Quockisister 2001). *Quathiaski Cove* is one of a number of First Nations names that are ascribed a variety of meanings, perhaps a reflection of population shifts in the region. George Quocksister, a Lekwala speaker, approximates the English spelling as Quait-see, "something to pee in." The name describes a rock formation just inside Whiskey Point that is shaped like a chamber pot. A Salish translation is "place in north side of point (from Cape Mudge)" (Galois1994: 270). An unnamed source gave the meaning as "island in mouth." *Cape Mudge* was named in 1792 for Vancouver's first lieutenant, Zachary Mudge. *Gowlland Harbour* was named for John Thomas Gowlland, R.N., engaged in surveys of this coast in the 1860s. The harbour was known by the First Nations people as gwigwakulis, which has been translated to "whale between the two" (Galois 1994: 270).

South Quadra Island

Cape Mudge – A Contemporary First Nations Village

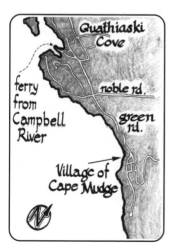

How to Get There: The Lekwiltok Village of the We-Wai-Kai people, at Cape Mudge, has been in use for several thousand years or more. To reach the village, turn right on Green Road, off the exit from the Quathiaski Cove ferry terminal.

Johnny Wilson, Ernest Price, Herman Quocksister, Bill Roberts, Norman Price, and another boy pose in feast dishes used at potlatches, large gatherings called to mark the major events of life for the First Nations people. In 1922, a government law banning potlatching was enforced and all dance and ceremonial regalia were seized. After years of lobbying, the government returned family possessions in 1979, to be housed at the Kwagiulth Museum at Cape Mudge Village. **MCR 10389, Henderson Collection.**

Lekwiltok warriors were known throughout Georgia Strait for their daring bravado. They were variously described in early journals as "fierce and bloodthirsty men" and the "fear inspiring Youkiltas." To protect themselves from reprisals, the Lekwiltok group living at Cape Mudge, the We-Wai-Kai, kept a stout palisade around their village. The British navy blasted this barricade asunder in the 1860s, in retaliation for a Lekwiltok attack on a Hudson's Bay Company messenger who passed through Discovery Passage.

This same vigilant protection of their territorial rights brought a coast-wide smallpox epidemic into the village in 1862. When a group of Haida people entered the passage, the We-Wai-Kai attacked and unwittingly picked up small-pox from the infected Haidas. Within two years of the outbreak of this disease in Victoria, one third of the Native population of BC was dead. Other diseases also took a heavy toll, including measles, mumps, diphtheria, and tuberculosis. A geological surveyor estimated there were 16 houses at the We-Wai-Kai village in 1878; by the mid-1880s there were only 11.[7] When the first official census was taken in 1881, only three of the seven original Lekwiltok tribes remained.

A forceful leader emerged from the general ranks of the We-Wai-Kai in the 1890s, guiding his people through a difficult transition. Chief Billy Assu, a man with a powerful intellect, introduced astute changes that allowed the We-Wai-Kai people to bridge the widening gap between their traditional culture and the emerging Euro-Canadian market economy. During his tenure, the Band started their own logging operation, and he was instrumental in the government's decision to overturn a law that barred Native people from working on seine boats.

As a young man, Assu supported the Band's request for a school and teacher, to be provided by the Methodist Mission. The first permanent missionaries to respond were Robert and Agnes Walker, who started a school in the village in 1893. Years later, in 1931, the We-Wai-Kai people named their new church in honour of Mr. Walker, who served the mission for over a decade. The church, meticulously restored by the current multi-denominational congregation, is at the centre of the village, along with a day care and a community hall/gymnasium.

Near the church is a cemetery where the oldest known grave is that of Harry Geeson, who died in August 1890. Another headstone marks the grave of Qua-Quock-Gilles (Wawmish), a great leader among the various Lekwiltok tribes. Wawmish saw, and attempted to resist, the sweeping change of his generation. His life spanned a time when this territory was exclusively under the control of Lekwiltok chiefs in the 1840s, to the proliferation of Euro-Canadian settlements scattered throughout the district in 1903. "He was much honoured," says this grand chief's headstone, "and respected by his own people; he was industrious as a canoe maker and a fisherman; and was charitable and good to his people; and a peacemaker among all the neighbouring tribes."

In 2001, there were 811 registered We-Wai-Kai Band members, with approximately 200 people living on the reserve at Cape Mudge. The Kwagiulth Museum at the centre of the village has an outstanding display of potlatch regalia dating back into the nineteenth century. Much of it was confiscated by the Canadian government in the 1920s, when a law banning potlatches was enforced and the We-Wai-Kai people's dance regalia was seized. After years of lobbying by First Nations elders, the federal government returned what remained of the collection in 1979. Many pieces had been sold in the intervening years. In addition to displays of the potlatch collection, the Kwagiulth Museum offers a fine selection of contemporary art and books in their gift shop. A new addition to the complex is an artists' carving studio, where visitors can see traditional arts and crafts in production.

An Ancient Village Site at Tsa-Kwa-Luten Lodge

How to Get There: Tsa-Kwa-Luten Lodge, owned and operated by the We-Wai-Kai Band, is adjacent to a former summer village of the Island Comox. The village was strategically positioned in a dramatic setting, high atop white sand cliffs looking over Georgia Strait and Discovery Passage. Follow the signs for Tsa-Kwa-Luten Lodge, off

Lighthouse Road. From the lodge parking lot, walk along the service road to the beach. At the crest of the hill, you'll find a foot path leading to the bluffs and a network of trails to forest walks, view points, and the beach.

Both Captain Vancouver and Dr. Archibald Menzies, of the *Discovery*, wrote detailed accounts of their visit, estimating the population was between 300 to 350 people:

> *After dinner, accompanied by Mr. Menzies and some of the officers, I went on shore to return the visit of our friends, and to indulge our curiousity. On landing at the village we were received by a man who appeared to be the chief of the party. He approached us alone, seemingly with a degree of formality, though with the utmost confidence of his own security, whilst the rest of the society, apparently numerous, were arranged and seated in the most peaceable manner before their houses.*
> Captain George Vancouver

> *Like the generality of Natives we met with in this Country these were of a middling stature & rather slender bodied of a light copper colour: they were awkward in their motions and ill formed in their limbs which no doubt in some measure proceeded from their constant practise of squatting down on their heels in their posture of setting either on Shore or in their Canoes: They have flat broad faces with small starting eyes: – Their Teeth are small & dirty; their Ears are perforated for appending Ornaments either of Copper or pearly Shells; the Septum of the Nose they also pierce & sometimes wear a quill or such quantity of red-ocre grease & dirt puffed over at times with white down that its real colour is not easily distinguishable; they have long black Beards with long Hair about their privates, but none on their Breasts or on the Arm Pits. – Some had ornamented their faces by painting it with red ocre sprinkled over with black Glimmer that helped not a little to heighten their ferocious appearance.*
> Dr. Archibald Menzies

Captain Vancouver wrote a detailed account of his visit to the village atop the steep, sandy bank at Cape Mudge in 1792. "Close to the edge of this precipice stood the village, the houses, not exceeding ten or twelve feet in height, close together in rows. On the beach, at the foot of the cliff, were about seventy canoes." A 15-year-old seaman, Sykes, who remained aboard ship, drew this sketch. It did not come to light in British Naval records until the 1980s. **MCR 18089.**

On the beach below Tsa-Kwa-Luten Lodge are 54 petroglyphs, images from the distant past pounded into the seaward surfaces of large and small boulders. Some represent abstract images of birds, animals, and humans; others are covered with countless circular "peck holes," following vaguely discernable patterns. Little is known about the purpose and meanings of these carvings. Some feel they were used in shamanic rituals, while others believe they represent family crests, magic ancestors, and spirit helpers.

Sea levels have been gradually rising over the preceding centuries, making it necessary to visit the petroglyphs at low tide. They are only visible in the early morning or evening, when the light slants across the boulders, highlighting the fading images. The most dramatic way to see them is on a dark night using a strong spotlight. Whenever you go, be prepared to search the beach methodically, starting with the largest of the smooth granite boulders facing the sea. Step back 10 metres (6 feet) or more to view the petroglyphs from a variety of angles. An interesting cluster of carvings can be found on large granite boulders directly off the mouth of the stream that cuts the old village site in two. Making rubbings or other impressions of these petroglyphs is strictly prohibited, but at the Kwagiulth Museum in the village at Cape Mudge cast impressions of petroglyphs are available for rubbing.

On the seaward side of the road approaching Tsa-Kwa-Luten, a stone's throw to the north of the lodge, is an old steam donkey the We-Wai-Kai people used for logging many decades ago. The impressive iron frame and boiler are just visible from the road. It requires a bit of bushwhacking through the ferns and broken ground to have a closer look.

Place Names: *Tsa-Kwa-Luten* may have been the original Salish place name, meaning "Indian-game place" (Kennedy and Bouchard 1984:169) for the current village site at Cape Mudge. A Lekwiltok elder, James Smith, gave the meaning as "cold spring of water" (Galois 1994: 275), and George Quocksister, a Lekwala speaker (Lekwiltok language), gives a closer approximation to English as Tsul-qua-luten-ay, which translates to "warm side of the island." *Cape Mudge:* Captain George Vancouver named it in 1792 for his 21-year-old first lieutenant, Zachary Mudge. *Discovery Passage:* Captain Vancouver named it for his ship, the *Discovery*.

Cape Mudge Lighthouse

How to Get There: Follow the signs for Tsa-Kwa-Luten Lodge and continue to the end of Lighthouse Road. The light station is not normally open to the public, but a footpath skirts around it, leading southward to Tsa-Kwa-Luten Lodge. The 90-minute return walk to the lodge, along flat ground, offers views of Discovery Passage, Campbell River, and the Vancouver Island mountains.

Discovery Passage has been an important sea route since ancient times, when First Nations people from as far away as the Queen Charlotte Islands raided and traded along the coast. The perilous shoals off Cape Mudge and the adjacent Willow Point reef have long commanded the respect of mariners. Two wrecks of the early 1890s, both of which resulted in loss of life, may have given rise to a plea for a lighthouse at the cape.

In June 1892, the cannery tug *Standard*, owned by John Irving and R.P. Rithet of Victoria, went down with the loss of five men. The sole survivor, chief engineer Murray, drifted for 15 hours on a small door. An eyewitness who tried unsuccessfully to reach the shipwreck said the waves were so high it was like climbing the sides of a mountain. A government agent in Comox described the wreck: "I beg to inform you that on Monday night, Dan and three other Cape Mudge Indians brought in the body of a man they found in the kelp near the Indian reservation and reported that a steamer sank off the Cape. M. King came in a canoe with Mr. Murray, the only survivor of the lost boat..." A few years later, a logging camp operator who was on the scene during the wreck of the *Standard,* a man named McDougall, also perished off Cape Mudge in the wreck the

Estelle. McDougall and seven shipmates vanished without a trace. The splintered fragments of the ship found throughout Discovery Passage and Johnstone Strait suggested the *Estelle* had suffered a massive explosion.

The Cape Mudge lighthouse was erected just in time to serve as a beacon for a parade of ships of all shapes and sizes, making their way to the Yukon Gold Rush. Young Katie (Walker) Clarke, child of the missionaries at the We-Wai-Kai village, remembered the wonder of seeing so much activity. Dogs barked as the boats passed, and sometimes fog-bound travelers stopped to share news of the outside world.

Katie also remembered every dish that was brought to the settlers' first community picnic, held on the grounds of the unfinished lighthouse in 1897. She and the other children ran about getting acquainted, enjoyed the rare treat of fancy food, foot races, and tea brewed over a beach fire. When the crowd gathered to sing "God Save the Queen," it was a high point of the picnic. "And I doubt it was sung

The Cape Mudge Lighthouse went into operation in 1898, warning ships away from the dangerous reef and powerful tidal action off the Cape. **MCR 2836, Easterbrook Collection.**

more lustily anywhere in the whole realm," recalled Katie Clarke many decades later.

Cape Mudge lightkeepers have come to the aid of numerous shipwreck victims over the years. The first keeper, John Davidson, flagged survivors of the *Cottage City* into a little cove to the north of the light, leading 14 women and a four-year-old boy through deep snow to the warmth of his home. "They were all very cold and i gave them all a little hote rum and they were soon all right and then the men was comen," reported the semi-literate Scotsman in his official report.

The **Cottage City** *was wrecked off Cape Mudge in 1911; though the passengers were badly shaken, there was no loss of life. Like the* **Northwestern,** *which went down more than a decade later, the* **Cottage City** *was enroute to the Yukon in a blinding snowstorm.* **MCR 7628, Joyce Collection.**

A near disaster was averted in 1927 when the American ship *SS Northwestern* ran aground on the shoals at Cape Mudge in a blinding snowstorm. The ship was on a Christmas run, taking 187 passengers and 450 kilograms (1,000 pounds) of freight (china, canned goods, gumboots, eggs, turkeys, chickens, cows, sacks of flour, and bales of hay) to Alaska. Area residents were roused from their beds at 5 a.m. to come to the aid of the stranded ship; though the seas were still running high, all the passengers were safely evacuated. The *Northwestern*'s freight became Christmas bounty for the cash-poor settlers, who pillaged the ship, hiding mismatched gum boots and cans of coffee and lard in their walls and beneath floorboards.

In recent years Jim Abram, the current lightkeeper, has waged a steady fight to maintain Cape Mudge as a staffed station. He is supported by pleas from mariners and pilots who rely on Abram's on-the-spot weather reports and his ability to provide immediate response to distress calls. While the Liberal government has agreed to no further destaffing, the bleating fog warning installed as part of the automation process has become a symbol of cultural loss for the people of Discovery Passage, who miss the deep, resonant booming of the old foghorn.

Maple Bank Farm

How to Get There: Alfred Joyce was among the first wave of non-Native settlers on Quadra Island, taking up choice land at the end of Joyce Road on the south tip of the island. The Joyces' frame house, a proud replacement of their original log cabin, has been preserved as a pottery studio and showroom by the current owners, Martha Nickoloff and Gordon James. A sign posted at the head of the driveway indicates when the studio is open to the public.

Alfred Joyce was a British immigrant, trained as a carpenter and plasterer. In 1889, he claimed a property neighbouring his brother Walter's pre-emption. And a few years later, while on a work stint in Victoria, he met and married Anna Walsh. Anna had a worldly background, having been raised in Switzerland and educated in New York, before travelling with friends to San Francisco and

Victoria, where she took a job as a waitress. The young couple were married in October 1892 and set off immediately for Quadra Island. Anna's first year must have been a trial. She arrived at the start of the short stormy days of early winter, settling into a small log cabin surrounded by a partially cleared homestead. Although

there was one other non-Native woman on the island, she lived too far away to be a companion. Whatever Anna's initial response may have been, she made pioneer life a success, becoming a model gardener, homemaker, and friend to all who knew her.

Anna Joyce made a success of pioneer life, leaving behind a distinctly different life in Switzerland and New York to develop a farm from wilderness.
MCR 5684, Yeatman Collection.

Maple Bank, as the Joyces called their place, was one of the most productive farms on the island. They raised beef and dairy cattle, sheep, and poultry, and grew a profusion of vegetables, flowers, and fruit.

In a typical coastal pattern, Anna Joyce maintained the farm and cared for their children on her own for many months of the year while Alfred followed his trade in distant communities. In a speech at a community gathering in 1906, Alfred said, "It is well known that my wife does most of the farming, at least, she thinks so, for she generally bosses the job, and I must admit that she is perfectly capable of doing it."[8]

Alfred died in 1927, but Anna lived on until 1954. An unmarried son, Arthur, stayed on at Maple Bank for a few years after her death. When he left, the old house stood vacant and the farm fields were tended by a brother living on a neighbouring farm. Three decades later, Gordon James and Martha Nickoloff purchased Maplebank and refurbished the old house to become a pottery studio and showroom open to the public.

The gnarled orchard at Maple Bank, encompassing several acres of grassy field, continues to produce an abundance of fruit. In this inspiring setting, overlooking Georgia Strait and the mountains of Vancouver Island, images of plums, hoary thistles, apples, ripe blackberries, and snow-capped mountains find their way into the design elements of Martha's and Gordon's pottery.

Kay Dubois Trail

How to Get There: North trailhead is at the end of Wa-wa-kie Road and the south access is at the end of Sutil Road. This 2-kilometre (1.2-mile) trail takes an easy 1-2 hours. Starting from the Sutil Road trailhead, you head through second-growth and switchback down a slight grade to a cobble beach. Going down the bank, look for the active Bald Eagle nest in the veteran Douglas-fir. The easy walking trail follows an old road grade just in from the beach, and there are five access points out to great views of the Coast Mountains, and Mitlenatch, Marina, Cortes, and Read Islands. Often, eagles soar overhead and sea ducks cavort offshore. You pass several old Sitka Spruce in amongst the second-growth Douglas-fir and Alder.

Ferns along the trail include Sword, Lady, Oak, and Spiny Wood. Depending on the time of year, you might glimpse Chocolate Lily, Tiger Lily, Pacific Bleeding Heart as well as False Lily-of-the-Valley. Besides the Bracken and Stinging Nettles, there are a selection of berries from Thimbleberry to Salmonberry and Huckleberry. A multi-limbed Sitka Spruce, locally known as the Goblin Tree, marks the junction of a trail that leads up to Fox Road.

The Bryant Homestead

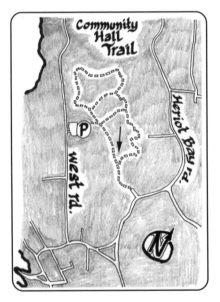

How to Get There: Directly behind the Community Centre, on West Road, is an old wagon road that has been incorporated into a network of well-marked hiking trails. Two-thirds of the way along the main trail is a fork leading to the vestiges of the Bryants' place, first settled in 1887. This easy walk takes about 45 minutes, return.

Marking the spot where the Bryants' squared log house once stood is a huge, spreading maple that lights the forest with a tremendous yellow glow in the fall. Nearby are a few shriveled fruit trees and traces of fallen house timbers.

Mary Bryant, the first non-Native woman to come to the island, outlived her husband by nearly 30 years. After her death, the property, considered a toilsome burden by the second generation, reverted to Crown land for back taxes. A few gnarled fruit trees and a massive maple tree are all that remain to mark the spot of her former home. **MCR 6825, Wargo Collection.**

"Black Jack Bryant," as he was called for his shock of black hair, fled the Nanaimo coal mines following a disastrous explosion in 1887 that took 147 lives. A series of Victoria newspaper articles promoting the many virtues of Quadra Island may have attracted the notice of Bryant and a few other disaffected miners. Jack and a partner, John Dauton Dixon, pre-empted Lot 123. Dixon took the southern half, with its massive trees and deep swamp, while Bryant took up the northern portion. Bryant immediately set to work draining a low-lying swamp in the centre of his claim, using a team of oxen to wrench stumps, roots and rocks from a network of trenches. Dixon, owner of a miner's inn and saloon at Wellington, must have decided against the backbreaking work of clearing his land for he never did settle on the island. The first-growth trees on Dixon's pre-emption were not logged until the year 2000, causing an anguished backlash among some island residents as the forest giants were felled.

There were only a handful of settlers on the island when Bryant and Dixon took out their pre-emption in 1887, all of them bachelors. About 100 We-Wai-Kai people lived at Cape Mudge, and a few logging camps scattered throughout the district provided work and a market for farm produce.

About a year after Jack Bryant moved to Quadra Island, he returned to his native Somerset, England, where he married his young cousin, Mary Sheppard. Jack left Mary in the comfort of his partner's inn at Wellington while he prepared his rustic 6-metre by 4-metre (20-foot by 14-foot) log cabin for his bride. When all was ready Mary followed, bringing six months of supplies, on a steamship that stopped at the nearest port of call at Comox. There Jack and a friend picked Mary and their provisions up in a huge war canoe borrowed from the We-Wai-Kai people, then paddled up the coast to their new home in the wilderness.[9]

To augment their rural income, Black Jack shod and drove ox teams in the logging camps for much of the spring and summer seasons, leaving Mary to manage the homestead. As a gregarious, fun-loving, person she must have experienced inexpressible loneliness. In 1889, Mary was the only English-speaking woman living on the island, surrounded by dense forest on a partially cleared farm. If some of the romanticized stories about Mary's early experiences can be credited, she had a great fear of the Lekwiltok people. Tales of their warlike feats had become almost legendary by the 1880s. Just prior to Mary's arrival, the newspapers were full of the overblown drama of two trials in which Lekwiltok men were charged with the brutal murders of settlers in Nanaimo and whiskey traders near Kelsey Bay. Mary is said to have kept a log barricaded against her door, watching in terror as the curious Native people peered in at her cabin windows. "One morning looking out from the cabin," recounted one of Mary's contemporaries, "she saw two squaws examining her washing ... the sombre maidens wished to exchange their garments for the fine lingerie made in England."[10] But, as Mary recalled in later years, her fears were unfounded, for the aboriginal people proved to be her neighbours and friends.

Mary Bryant's first pregnancy was at term in the winter of 1890, a year that still holds the record for heavy snowfall. With the snow lying deep in the forests and deeper still in the logged-over clearings, the Bryants made their way to Cape Mudge Village just weeks prior to Mary's due date. The We-Wai-Kai people loaned them a canoe for the trip to Comox, where they awaited a southbound steamship for Wellington. Their son, William, was born on January 31, 1890, in a room at the Somerset Inn. Five weeks later, with the snow at depths of 1.8 metres (6 feet) or more and still falling, the Bryants returned to Quadra, prevailing upon a coastal steamer to let them disembark in mid-passage into a canoe from the Cape Mudge Village. They camped at the village in a deserted logger's shack before making their way to the nearest settler's cabin; they stayed for two weeks, unable to go any further until the weather eased enough to make the walk home possible.

Mary and her infant son thrived despite this taxing start. Diarist and early Campbell River settler, Fred Nunns, sometimes mentioned his friends the Bryants in his journal of 1890:

> *Sunday 20 July: Got up late and was just busy cleaning the house when Mr. & Mrs. Jack Bryant, baby and Tom Backus came in. Luckily I was able to give them a good dinner, pickles, salmon, bacon, poached eggs and potatoes.*

Sunday 14 December: I was getting ready to go to Black Jack's when Smith Thompkins came up with his 'missus' and two others. He stayed about 20 minutes and then we went over to the Cove in company. Just as we got there rain came on again. Got up to the Bryant's wet through. Found them quite well, baby grown a fine child.[11]

The Bryants stayed put on Quadra Island for the birth of their second child, assisted by a newcomer, Alice Pidcock, who served as a midwife for her fellow settlers. Daisy Bryant was proudly heralded in an 1892 Victoria newspaper as the first white child to be born on Quadra Island.

The Bryants made many improvements to their property over time. They replaced Jack's bachelor shack with a more substantial log house and created a garden their contemporaries remembered as one of the prettiest on the island. But their farm, which had always been marginal, was left a smoking ruin in a fire that swept through the middle of the island in 1919. The boggy soil of Jack's hard-won farm field burnt for a long time, leaving it a charred waste that returned to swamp.

In spring, the Bryant's pond is a riot of frog song. Swamps like this attracted the first settlers, who dug deep drainage trenches to expose thick, black soil.

Black Jack Bryant died in 1922, leaving Mary a widow for the remainder of her long life. In 1939, the community celebrated her 50th year on the island with a party at the community hall. Although crippling arthritis kept Mary confined to a chair, a newspaper report of the day said she was nonetheless "the gayest of them all." Mary passed away at the age of 89 in 1950, after which her property reverted to Crown land for non-payment of taxes. The farm field, where Jack's deep trenches can still be seen, has reverted to a vast marsh, filled with flowering shrubs and birdsong.

The Haskins' Farm Trail

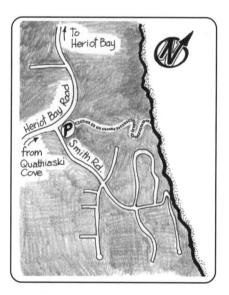

How to Get There: At the Heriot Bay and SmithRoad junction there is a sign for the Haskins' Farm Trail, which winds through a second-growth forest of Western Hemlock and Douglas-fir, before opening to an abandoned meadow and orchard. The trail continues through a woodlot, down a steep bank, to a rocky beach with a view of islands and mountains. This 2.5-kilometre (1.5-mile) trail can be easily walked in 1-2 hours.

A visit to the Haskins' orchard can be combined with a walk along the Bryants' trail, which terminates at Heriot Bay Road. From the end of the Bryants' trail, walk north on the roadside path to the junction of Smith and Heriot Bay Roads, where the Haskins' trail begins.

Wilson and Brady had a railway logging show, with a track running through the centre of south Quadra Island from about 1910 to 1920. They dumped their logs in Drew Harbour, where a few random pilings remain on the beach across from the We-Wai-Kai Campground office. **MCR 20191 - 23, Noble Collection.**

George Haskins was a husky Englishman who registered his 84-hectare (212-acre) pre-emption in November 1893. Around 1911, Haskins sold the rights to his timber to the first and only railway logging outfit[12] to operate on the south end of Quadra Island. Their track ran through the centre of the island from Walker Road to a log dump on the We-Wai-Kai people's reserve in Drew Harbour. The Wilson and Brady Logging Company was burnt out in 1919[13] in a fire that destroyed several homesteads and many acres of trees. The Garats, recent immigrants from the south of France, were living in the company's tent camp when the fire broke out. John Garat, then a boy of nine, recalls that the camp was evacuated on rail cars covered over with wet canvas. To get the train through to Drew Harbour, the engineer, Ted Johnson, had to run the train in the direction of dense smoke and flying embers, straight into the oncoming fire. The rails ahead of them were buckling in the intense heat. "It was a do-or-die affair," recalls Garat, but Johnson got them through to the beach. The loggers and their families took over a deserted shack on the beach and settled in for the night, only to find themselves once again in peril, this time from a chimney fire that was quickly extinguished.

After years of toil on his place, Haskins enlisted for service in England at the outset of World War I, returning after the conflict with an English bride. For a time, Haskins augmented his income by working as a teamster at a copper mine in north Gowlland Harbour. "He walked to the camp and back every day," recalled a contemporary, the late Tommy Hall. "[It was] a long journey for someone who had to be the first one in camp every morning to harness and feed the horses."

George and Mary Haskins are said to have invested two inheritances in their farm, over a 30-year span, before giving up and moving to New Westminster. Long-time resident Grace (Willson) McPherson visited the property with prospective buyers shortly after the Haskins left. "They just picked up their bags and left—leaving everything as it was," she recalled. "The tea pot was still on the table full of tea."

In 1926, the Morton family of Sayward rented the property, intending to develop it into a dairy farm. Doug Morton recalled that the house was a simple log shack, but the barn was a remarkable structure made from massive logs that were so thick it only took four to make up a full wall. Within a few years, the Mortons also gave up on the place, and the farm reverted to Crown land for unpaid taxes.

In 1975, the abandoned farm made the national news when a vigilante group bulldozed squatters' shacks in the old clearing. Longtime resident Sam Hooley recalls the cause of alarm was a smoldering fire thought to have been left burning for several days. According to Hooley, some of the "young bucks" overreacted, pushing over the flimsy shacks of a photographer and a musician who were away from home. A third fellow, Al McLoughlin, was given notice to remove his belongings from his place before it was dismantled. A couple of young men, recalls Hooley, hung nooses in the trees, serving notice to the squatters that they must not return. It was the nooses that captivated the imagination of the national media.

Ted Mather, then a newcomer to the island, says the story was blown out of proportion, but it did bring about a positive end result. For a number of years, tension had been mounting between longtime residents and the hippies. After the nooses made their appearance on national television, many of those involved were disturbed by how their actions were perceived. Ted recalls this as the turning point in community relations. "Suddenly all the rednecks were really nice to me, going out of their way to show they were not like they were portrayed on television."

Group of Quadra residents c. 1916, including George Haskins far right. **MCR 7067 Ferguson Collection.**

The property is now part of a woodlot, a managed forest being selectively harvested by island residents, Alex and Ellen Hartford. The Hartfords give a wide berth to the hiking trail, much-used by horseback riders, walkers, and cyclists.

Quadra Island Cemetery

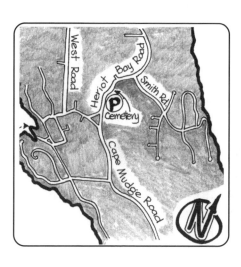

How to Get There: When 16-year-old Alice Bryant died from diphtheria in June 1913, the non-Native community was galvanized into action to establish a cemetery. Previously, settlers and loggers were simply buried where they died. The quaint little Quadra Island cemetery is located on Heriot Bay Road, just north of the Cape Mudge Road junction. A visit to the cemetery can be incorporated into a walk along the Bryant trail, which terminates at Heriot Bay Road. From there it is a 10-minute walk south along Heriot Bay Road to the cemetery.

The graveyard is a blend of old and new headstones, a time capsule of the island's non-Native history. A few years after the cemetery was officially opened in 1915, Alice Bryant's remains were moved to a family plot. A headstone that may have been placed there some years later inaccurately named her death date as the year she was disinterred. Nearby is the grave of another pioneer, who went missing while hunting near Duncan Bay in 1903. Frederick Yeatman's remains were not found until some years after his accidental death and eventually moved to the little cemetery. Alice Pidcock's tall headstone stands in the middle of the old part of the cemetery, in the north quadrant. After a life of pioneering in various places on north Vancouver Island, Alice's large family moved to Quathiaski Cove, where they built a sawmill, store, and cannery.

Both "Skookum Tom" and Maggie Leask of Hyacinthe Bay died prematurely, a few years apart, and their children were sent to a Vancouver orphanage. One of the boys sickened and died almost immediately and was returned to the island to be buried beside his parents. **MCR 6049, Joyce Collection.**

In the early years, the Quadra Island cemetery served for the entire region. Many of the off-islanders interred were men from no known address, victims of logging accidents. Like Czarlo Lodryk (alias Charles Woodrick), who died on the job in Loughborough Inlet in 1916, they were often buried in unmarked graves. According to his workmates, Lodryk was Russian and had been in camp for 36 days; all other details on his death certificate were simply marked "don't know."

Chinese men who died while seasonally employed at the cannery in Quathiaski Cove also rested in unmarked graves. In some cases after the next of kin were located, the remains were disinterred and shipped to China, but a few cannery workers are thought to still remain in the northeast section of the cemetery.

Others in the old quadrant include the Joyce family and legendary strong-man "Skookum Tom" Leask, a widower who drowned in 1927. His young family had to be turned over to an orphanage in Vancouver, but most eventually returned. Countess de Almedia Portugal was a British aristocrat who served as a lady-in-waiting to Queen Victoria before retiring to her daughter's home on distant Quadra Island.

In the newer part of the cemetery, to the south, are the graves of people whose names have been honoured in community parks and organizations. Phil Thompson, a warm-hearted character, beloved of children, has a day care named in his memory. Blenkin Park was named for a family killed in a car accident while on a summer holiday in Alberta in 1961.

Rebecca Spit Marine Provincial Park

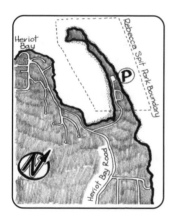

How to Get There: Rebecca Spit Marine Provincial Park, with its hiking trails, swimming beach, and views of the outer islands and mainland mountains, is the premier beauty spot on Quadra Island. Follow the signs for the park, which is on the east side of the island, off Heriot Bay Road. The spit is a long, narrow neck of land that curves toward Heriot Bay, forming the protected anchorage of Drew Harbour, a favoured spot for summer boaters. While the park itself is restricted to day use, the We-Wai-Kai Band operates a well-appointed campground at the entrance to the park.

Watching seabirds provides year-round pleasure at Rebecca Spit. During the fall and winter, rafts of Scoters, Goldeneye, and Bufflehead feed in Drew Harbour. Harlequin and Long-tailed Ducks are often found diving off the end of the spit. Plants include Salal, Dull Oregon-grape, Nootka Rose, Snowberry, Oceanspray, Indian-pipe, Saskatoon, Western Trumpet Honeysuckle, Harvest Brodiaea, Nodding Onion, Fawn Lily, and Chocolate Lily.

The long curve of Rebecca Spit forms Drew Harbour, a protected waterway that served as a refuge and food gathering site for the First Nations people for hundreds of years. Drew Creek (which they called Tsatsahesin, "place with plenty of gravel"),[14] was an important salmon fishing station until the last century and as such was allocated as a reserve to the We-Wai-Kai people in 1879. Around the corner in Heriot Bay is an extensive shell midden that suggests the bay was once a major winter village; on the spit itself was a small defended retreat used during times of warfare.

A defensive site used in ancient times by the First Nations people, seen to the left, at the first treeless opening on the spit, was the subject of the only archaeological dig in our region. Tree core samples helped to establish that the place was last used over 400 years ago.

This latter site was the subject of an archaeological dig in 1966. Archaeologists determined there were three to four small houses on this knoll at the north end of the first tree-less opening on the spit, surrounded by a palisade and 1.3-metre (4-foot) deep trenches. The 137 stone and bone tools found are thought to be from one assemblage that included knives, scrapers, harpoons, wedges, a beaver tooth engraver, and a large clam shell used as a container for red ochre paint. The midden deposits showed that the refuge was last used about 400 years ago. The people lived on shellfish, salmon, rockfish, Harbour Seal, deer, and racoon. A footpath now cuts down into the black soil of one of the trenches at this site.

From the earliest years of European settlement, Drew Harbour was a favoured anchorage for traders, whiskey peddlers and the British Navy, which made a show of strength by practicing manoeuvres in the harbour. In 1882, Victoria entrepreneurs began buying up the land surrounding Drew Harbour. In the spring of 1884, the Colonist newspaper reported that a logging camp was being hauled up coast to Drew Harbour. A few months later the same paper said 123,000 metres (400,000 feet) of logs had been hauled from Drew Harbour to Sayward's Mill in Victoria. The spit itself seems to have been left unscathed. In 1887, William Sayward bought the land, but he may have simply used it for a camp. No evidence of early logging is visible.

Just before World War I, a logging outfit persuaded the We-Wai-Kai Band to sell off part of their timber in Drew Harbour. The Band also allowed an easement for a rail line running through the reserve to a log dump in the harbour. According to the late Harry Assu, the We-Wai-Kai refused Wilson and Brady's offer of $5,000 for their timber rights but when the head men were away fishing, the Indian agent persuaded 11 Band members (all but one of whom were illiterate) to sign away their rights. A few years later, the Band logged the remainder of their land at Drew Harbour on their own, making a handsome profit that allowed them to build new homes in their village at Cape Mudge.[15]

By 1905, the spit had become a chicken ranch, in the hands of Robert Kelly. A later owner, Maxwell, allowed the community to hold their annual May Day picnics on his property. Almost 100 years later the spit is still the favoured place for this old-fashioned celebration. The event includes the crowning of the May Queen, May Pole dancers, foot races, and a contest to climb a greased pole.

"The whole Island," wrote Eve (Willson) Eade in her memoirs, "would gather at the spit for the big celebration on the 24th of May. There were sports and games, the crowning of the May Queen. Then a long line of tablecloths would be laid out on the grass and the picnic lunch shared by everyone. At night there would be a dance at the community hall." May Day picnic, 1902. Photographer: John Hood. MCR 4363, Yeatman Collection.

James Clandening purchased the spit sometime before 1917, moving into an old log house there in the early 1930s. He later built a frame house near the current entrance to the park and opened a commercial machine shop. The Clandenings were on hand for the massive earthquake of

June 23, 1946, measuring 7.2 on the Richter Scale. Their land was ripped open in great slashes, and the tip of the spit slumped into the sea.

In 1958, the Clandenings accepted a government offer of a land swap and some cash to secure the property as a park. For the first few years, Rebecca Spit was used for both camping and picnicking, a favoured place by residents and boaters. Latterly, it has been restricted to day use to protect the delicate ecology.

Easy hiking trails make a circuit around the spit, and a boat launch is located near the entrance to the park. This is an excellent access point for exploring by small boat, in relatively protected waters. A number of kayak guiding and rental operations using Drew Harbour are located near the Heriot Bay shopping plaza. An afternoon or evening

The earthquake of June 23, 1946 measured 7.2 on the Richter scale. The tip of Rebecca Spit slumped into the sea and gaping chasms ripped open throughout. At the south end of the island, on what is now Terra Nova Farm, Herbert Joyce leapt from his tractor as the expansive farm field heaved in arching waves. **MCR 12965, Clandening Collection.**

paddle to the Breton Islands, visible off the north tip of the spit, is a popular outing.

Place Names: *Drew Harbour* was named by Captain Pender, a British surveyor, for Charles Randolph Drew, R.N., who was stationed on the BC coast from 1868-1871 (Walbran 1971: 151). The original Kwakwaka'wakw name was Tsatsahesin, "place with plenty of gravel" (Galois 1994: 274), while the Salish name for the harbour translates to "bent over back" (Kennedy and Bouchard 1990: 443). *Rebecca Spit* was named by Captain Pender, c. 1864, for the British trading schooner *Rebecca*, engaged on this coast for several years (Walbran 1971: 418-419).

Heriot Bay Inn

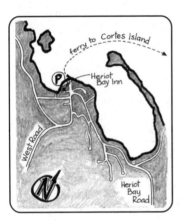

How to Get There: The Heriot Bay Inn is one of the few remaining examples of the old style hotels that were once a common feature of logging camp settlements on the coast. Follow the signs for the Cortes Island ferry dock, at the north end of West Road.

Hosea Bull bought 64 hectares (160 acres) in Heriot Bay in about 1895, having formerly worked (according to varying reports) as a bookkeeper, a preacher, and a cannery night watchman in Steveston. He arrived on the island with his wife Cordelia and a year later they adopted an infant, Cecil Bull.

The Bulls were classic entrepreneurs, high energy people who transformed their remote home into a bustling hive of activity. "When I first saw Heriot Bay there was a logging camp on the spot, and the forest around was one of the heaviest timbered ones on this side of the island," recalled Bull in a speech in 1906.[16] Bull ran his own logging camps, and within a few short years he opened a store, sawmill, and hotel, which became the nucleus of the largest community in the district, with its own government wharf and post office.

The first Heriot Bay Hotel, opened in about 1895,[17] was a log and frame structure located somewhat to the east of the current building. It was a place of few pretensions, a "loggers' watering hole," disdained by the island's elite. One of the regulars was Tom Leask, a guide, packer, and logger with a fine homestead in Hyacinthe Bay. Leask's wiry strength earned him the Chinook jargon nickname "Skookum Tom." Legend has it he had a double set of teeth that he used to impress one and all by chewing up beer glasses. Leask figures in several tales of fights at the Heriot Bay Hotel. On one occasion, he fought a beefy opponent for over two hours before the fight was postponed until daylight. Leask, bruised and swollen, lay down on the spot, but his opponent left for more comfortable quarters, which was his undoing for he was unable to drag himself back to resume the fight.

The self-styled "Lord Hughie Horatio Nelson Baron Bacon" was also a regular at the Heriot Bay Hotel. A prankster named Charlie Hall had some fun with Lord Bacon when he arrived one night packing a .45, ready for a shoot-out with a man named Hannager. Charlie got the bartender to double up on Bacon's drinks, and before long he was out cold and firmly tied down in a bed upstairs. When Hannager arrived packing a long-barrel .44, he was treated in the same manner; before long he too was out cold and strapped in place alongside Lord Bacon. When the two men came to and discovered their predicament, their shouts at each other quickly turned on their friends as they threatened to burn down the hotel. "They was so set on revenge," recalled an old-timer, "that they forgot their feud and never did get around to having a shoot-out."

Helen Bull transformed the Heriot Bay Hotel from a loggers' saloon into a refined establishment frequented by summer visitors. They enjoyed an aviary, tennis lawn and top-floor dance hall, where only the sober were admitted. **MCR 20126 - 90, McAllister Collection.**

Cordelia Bull passed away prematurely in 1905, and within about a year Hosea married a widow named Helen. The "second Mrs. Bull" had prior experience in the hotel business. She injected a more sophisticated style into the management of the Heriot Bay Hotel, building it up into a tourist resort. In December 1911, they opened a new hotel with a separate dining room for their summer visitors, at a suitable distance from the "snake pit," the loggers' bar. But within months of opening, the hotel was destroyed by fire, leaving only the chimney and a smoking ruin of upthrust bed frames. The Bulls quickly replaced the hotel, parts of which remain in the current structure.

Things went well for the Bulls until the long, dragged-out recession caused by World War I began to take its toll in the early 1920s. The Bulls' experience was harder than most, for Helen died of cancer in December 1924, and within months Hosea went into receivership, losing everything to his creditors. He disappeared into poverty in Vancouver, where he was last seen selling blankets on a street corner.

The hotel went through a string of owners following the demise of the Bulls. In 1927, it was purchased by Charles and Beatrice Webster, a globe-trotting English family with a private income. The Websters took a dim view of drinking, so they dropped the hotel licence and converted the place into a private residence and store. To the dismay of many, who viewed the hotel as community property, they demolished the east wing with its elegant verandah.

In the late 1930s, Joseph Calwell bought the hotel through a ruse, from a man named Hundley. The two were not on good terms, so Calwell had a friend pose as the buyer, taking over after the deal was closed. Calwell's daughter-in-law, Midge, remembered seeing the beautiful old furniture, crystal, and china piled up in the disused hotel rooms. Much of it was dumped off the end of the wharf as the old place was slowly converted to a boarding house.

The Heriot Bay wharf resounded with the clump of loggers' boots as men came and went in a continual parade between "town" (Vancouver) and the camps of the outer islands. The Bull family kept the hotel open day and night, "even on Sundays," to welcome them. Seen here is the Union Steamship boat, Cheakamus, *in 1914.* **MCR 6339, Yeatman Collection.**

In 1943, the property was once again sold. The new owners made many structural changes while converting the building back into a hotel and bar. An old bunkhouse was skidded into place on the east side of the building, replacing the wing that had been dismantled in 1927. The current owners of the Heriot Bay Inn, as it is now called, have taken the Bulls' lead. They adroitly balance the needs of the local characters who habituate the bar with those of summer visitors. The pub, of a Saturday night, is still the favoured spot for the tellers of tales, while on the other side of the building summer visitors are served tasty meals amidst the flowers on the verandah that overlooks the islands and rocky shoreline of Heriot Bay.

Place Names: *Heriot Bay* was named in about 1862 by Captain Richards, a British surveyor, for Frederick Lewis Maitland Heriot, kinsman of Rear Admiral Maitland, commander-in-chief for the BC naval station (Walbran 1971: 240).

Hopespring Trail & Thompson Trail to Heriot Ridge

How to Get There: Take Hyacinthe Bay Road north from Heriot Bay and turn left on Hopespring Road. The 5-kilometre (3-mile) trail begins by the driveway at the end of the road and is a moderate 3-4 hour hike.

The trail climbs steadily to the ridge past Sword Ferns and head-high Devil's Club growing in the Red Alder and Douglas-fir. At the signpost, go right for views of Heriot Bay and the Discovery Islands, plus Vancouver Island and the mountains in Strathcona Park. Return to the signpost and head down to the Gowlland Harbour trail.

Look for old-growth Douglas-fir, some over 300 years old. Lady, Spiny Wood, Bracken, and Deer Fern can be found in the understory along with Vanilla Leaf and Pathfinder. Sedges and Skunk Cabbage grow in the wetlands. After the third bridge, follow signs for the Thompson trail to the right.

The trail winds its way back to Heriot ridge. Tiny red spots on some of the downed timber is the lichen Lipstick Cladonia. A short, marked, side trail takes you to a view-point over Hyacinthe Bay and Rebecca Spit. Once back on the trail, follow all signs now for Thompson Road. At Thompson Road, turn right and walk to the junction with Hopespring Road. Turn right opposite the medical clinic, and within 10 minutes you'll be back at your starting point.

North Quadra Island

Morte Lake Trail

How to Get There: Parking and trailhead is 0.7 kilometres (0.4 miles) west on Walcan Road from Hyacinthe Bay Road. The trail around the lake is about 6.5 kilometres (4 miles) and takes about 3 hours.

The Quadra Trails Committee built the Morte Lake Trail in 1986-7 with financial support from the treefarm licence holder. In 1990, a parcel of private land on the lake was put up for sale, and the Quadra Island Conservancy and Stewardship Society was formed to buy the property. After three years of community fundraising, the land was purchased for $180,000.

A Natural History Guide to the Morte Lake Trail (available at several outlets on the island) was produced by the Mitlenatch Field Naturalists Society to celebrate the event. An interesting feature of the guide is hints for recognizing different owls. "Barred Owl (hoot sounds like: 'who cooks for you'), Great Horned Owl ('Who whowhowho WHO WHO'), Northern Saw-whet Owl ('hoothoothoothoothoothoot...') and tiny Northern Pygmy Owl ('hoot...hoot...hoot...')."

On the western shore of the lake are the remains of a logging camp operated by the Thulin brothers of Campbell River in about 1920. The camp was in use long enough to take on the comforts of home, a patch of mint, fencing for the animals, and a bridge across Morte Lake stream. To the north of this stream are stacked rocks around old stumps, perhaps an attempt to rid the camp site of rocks. Gnome plants, salmon pink flowers with yellow centres, grow on the rocks. This plant lacks chlorophyll and derives its nutrients from a relationship with fungi. Watch out for the old garbage dump just behind this area, which is littered with broken glass and pottery. The Thulin brothers, who ran their logging operation at arms length while also managing hotels and stores in Lund and Campbell River, were not always practical businessmen. Old-timers still chuckle over the fact that the Thulins used four steam donkeys to haul logs from the lake to the ocean. The donkey boilers consumed double or more the number of logs they hauled along the ravished stream.

Chinese Mountains Trails

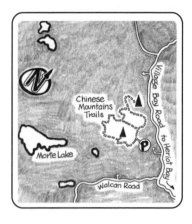

How to Get There: Turn off Hyacinthe Bay Road, 0.6 kilometres (0.3 miles) north of Walcan Road. The trailhead is 0.6 kilometre (0.3 mile) from the road. This hike to scenic lookouts takes 2-3 hours to hike 5 kilometres (3 miles). To get to the south peak, which has the best views, take the left trail at the fork at the trailhead. Almost 0.4 kilometres (0.2 miles) along the trail there is a junction. The left trail connects to the Morte Lake trail; follow the right for the summit. The trail quickly gains elevation, going in and out of second-growth deciduous/coniferous forest and along rocky bluffs. Just before the summit, the north-south connector trail joins the south peak trail. The view from South Chinese Mountain is spectacular, over the whole south end of Quadra.

To reach the north peak, take the right path at the fork at the trailhead. About 0.6 kilometres (0.3 miles)

View from the south peak toward Rebecca Spit

later, there is a junction: take the right path 1.2-kilometres (0.7-miles) up a steep trail to the top. At the peak, clumps of weather-worn Shore Pine give a sub-alpine atmosphere and views beckon over the Bretons and South Read Island. Often, Turkey Vultures are riding thermals near the summit in summer. Be aware—there are also ticks at this time.

Nugedzi Lake Trail

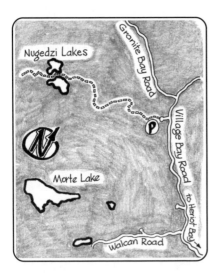

How to Get There: Head north on Hyacinthe Bay Road; after about 9 kilometres (5.4 miles) turn at Nugedzi Lakes signpost and park. Allow 4-6 hours for this moderate 7-kilometre (4.2-mile) hike as there is a stiff climb at the beginning.

The Mitlenatch Field Naturalists, which started with Roderick Haig-Brown as an honourary president back in the 1970s, did much of the initial work on this trail. The trail heads up an old logging road for an hour and then enters old-growth forest. At a sign post, a side trail heads east to a pond where a beaver dam has enlarged this picturesque body of water. This side trail continues on to a viewpoint over the Discovery Islands.

Back on the main trail, follow it through a forest of old-growth Douglas-fir and Western Redcedar underlain by a carpet of green moss to Nugedzi Lake. Running Clubmoss graces the open part of the trail and Slender Bog Orchid, Heart-leaved Twayblade, and Northwest Twayblade thrive in the old growth. Look for the loop boardwalk trail to Little Nugedzi Lake. In July, Western

False Asphodel and the carnivorous Round-leafed Sundew can be found around the shores of Little Nugedzi Lake. Beyond the lakes, continue west to the viewpoint over Discovery Passage and Vancouver

A section of trail in the oldgrowth

Island. Return the way you came to Little Nugedzi; if you have time, take the connecting trail to Mount Seymour.

Shellallagan Pass Trail

How to Get There: Head north from Heriot Bay, then turn down Valdez Road. Continue past Marina Road, and turn down a logging road at the woodlot sign. If you pass Breton Road, you've missed the logging road. Follow the logging road for 1.5 kilometres (0.9 miles) and park by the beach. In 2-4 hours of easy hiking you can cover the 3-5 kilometres (1.8-3 miles).

After skirting the rocky coastline, this ocean view trail comes back though mixed deciduous forest and harvested woodlot. The trail starts at a small bay with a beach that is great for picnics and fun for kids to explore when the tide is out. The trail continues over rocky headlands with views of Harlequin Ducks and cormorants in March. Stunted

Douglas-fir and Shore Pine (a coastal form of Lodgepole Pine, with twisted and bushy limbs) grow along the cliffs. Shore Pine has two needles to a bundle; Douglas-fir needles stick out around the twig.

There are two ways to return once you leave the coastline. Either head south through a fern forest and old logging road or continue north and cross a ravine back to the beach. Note all the oyster shells; further along you will see the floats from a commercial oyster lease. The trail then heads inland along a forested gully with a lovely creek. Once back onto the Village Bay Main Logging Road, head left and watch for the trail sign on your right to take you back to the woodlot road you drove in on. Turn left at this road to return to your car.

If you are lucky you might see Harbour Seals or sea lions along the Shellallagan Pass Trail.

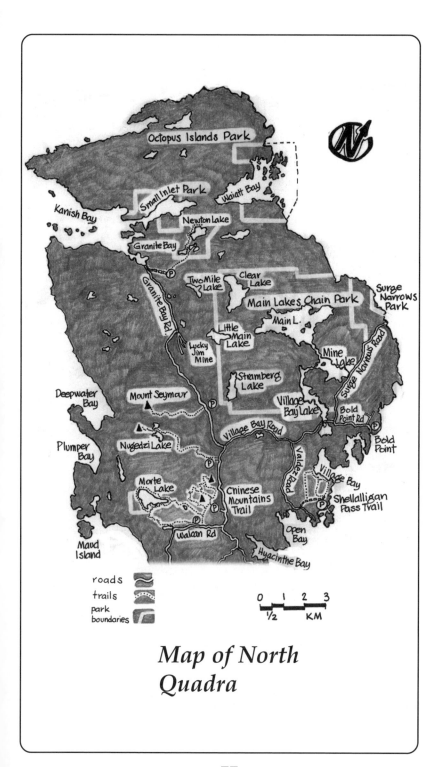

Map of North
Quadra

Village Bay and Main Lakes

How to Get There: The interconnected lake system on the north end of Quadra Island includes Village Bay, Mine

Canoeing the shallow channel between Village Bay Lake and Mine Lake

and Main Lakes, all of which offer excellent boating and swimming. Follow Hyacinthe Bay Road to Village Bay Road, a well-maintained dirt road, that leads to a bridge and boat ramp. There are summer cottages on this portion of the lake, visible from the Village Bay Lake bridge, where you'll find parking, outhouses, and a public telephone. Paddle north from the bridge through a narrow, reedy passage that leads to Mine Lake and Main Lake, a large body of water studded with islands. There is a 10 hp limit on Village Bay and Mine Lake, to preserve this wilderness environment. There is an alternate boat launch, with outhouses and parking on Mine Lake, about 4 kilometres (2.4 miles) along the Surge Narrows Road.

The lakes have many attractions. A hiking trail accessible from a northeast bay of Main Lake follows an old logging road down to the ocean at Yeatman Bay. The hike takes approximately 60 minutes return. In the northwest part of Main Lake, an undulating canoe track leads through tall, rustling bull rushes to Shadow Brook. Paddling to the north end of the lake may take longer than a day for inexperienced boaters, who should be prepared for strong breezes that can come up on this large lake. There are a few partially cleared camp sites on Main Lake, with no facilities. The lake system has many favourite swimming spots for islanders, who stay away from the muddy shallows favoured by leeches.

There was a considerable logging operation on Village Bay Lake early in the twentieth century. Moffat Brothers Logging had a floating camp at the lakes, where they boomed their logs before floating them through the dammed opening of Village Bay Creek. The dam allowed the Moffats to control the level of the lake, raising it considerably. There are persistent stories that a sunken tug

Donnie Haas lived on a floating logging camp on Village Bay Lake prior to 1920. He still remembers waking in the night to the sound of the floathouse creaking and shifting as it inexplicably settled onto dry land. By morning the house was sitting on a muddy hillside. The Native people, for whom Village Bay Creek was an important fishery, blew up the loggers' dam, dropping the lake to its original level. **BCARS F-0265.**

still lies at the bottom of the lake. A dam on Village Bay Creek was a serious detriment to fish stocks, a hereditary resource of the late Chief Billy Assu. His people once had a village, "Yakwen", at the outlet of the stream at Village Bay. To protect their fish stocks, the Native people blew up the loggers' dam in the dead of night, allowing the salmon to spawn.[18]

Little evidence remains of the former logging operation on Village Bay Lake, part of which was developed for summer cottages in the 1970s. Main Lake has limited privately owned land, part of which has recently been set aside as a park preserve.

Place Names: The First Nations name for *Village Bay* was "Yakwen". The name may actually pertain to the creek flowing into the bay. The meaning has been lost (Galois 1994: 275). *Sutil Channel* was named by Spanish explorers in 1792, meaning subtle.

Bold Point

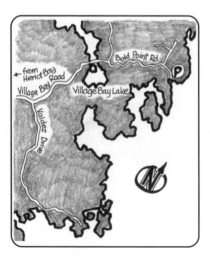

How to Get There: The dilapidated dock at Bold Point was last used in the 1950s, when the freight and passenger service of the Union Steamship Company ceased to operate. To get to Bold Point, take Hyacinthe Bay Road to Village Bay Lake, crossing over to Bold Point Road. Park at the end of the road to walk down the steep grade to the old wharf.

The trail passes the crumpled ruins of the former post office on the left and an orchard on the right.

The orchard was likely planted by the legendary Moses Cross Ireland, who was Bold Point's first non-Native resident. Ireland's life was full of adventure. He started out in logging, working the river drives in the State of Maine, and then migrated west to search for gold in California and later in the Cariboo. He became a partner in one of the first lumber mills in Burrard Inlet, which he gave up to start a freighting service on the Skeena River. An account of Ireland's life published just after his death said there were thousands who knew the old man, yielding him the respect accorded to heroes.

Ireland was about 54 when he gave up the rigors of packing for timber cruising and logging in the Cortes Island region in the early 1880s. It was a time of fast-paced speculation in timber holdings, when an experienced man could make easy money advising investors on profitable stands of timber. Ireland is still referred to in logging annals as the "father of timber cruisers," an elite class in the forest industry, able to provide complex knowledge of the value of timber based on species, locale, and logging methods.

Ireland also set up and ran his own logging camps from his base on the Camp Islands (now Subtle Islands), off the west coast of Cortes. For the first few years, he maintained winter quarters in Victoria, where he met and married a widow from Tennessee in 1888. A year, later Ireland bought his property at Bold Point. He may have intended it as a retirement haven, for it wasn't until 1901 that the couple settled there, operating a small hotel and post office, in addition to a cattle ranch.

Many sensational accounts of Ireland's life have been published over the years. Even his death, in 1913, gave rise to continuing tales. One of his contemporaries, a respected Justice of the Peace, recalled late in life that Ireland was the victim of an unsolved murder; and some area residents say his ghostly presence haunts his unmarked grave on the old ranch. But his death certificate gives a different account. It states that Ireland died of heart failure and was taken to Vancouver for burial. "His last days he spent in peace," said the Province newspaper in 1913, "not far from the big timber. When it came to bringing his body down to the city of Vancouver, the *Cassiar* made a stop just a trifle longer than usual for the freight from Bold Point. It was fitting that the *Cassiar* should have carried Mose Ireland, for he was a man of the woods, like most of the passengers on that hard-working vessel."

The Bell family and Roland Woolsey, a wrangler and cowhand, at the Bold Point ranch, weathered the Great Depression away from the expense of urban living, where Woolsey had been a jockey for a race course. **MCR 6751, Woolsey Collection.**

After Julia Ireland passed away in 1917, the Bell family took over the Bold Point Ranch and ran 120 head of cattle during the Depression. The hotel was no longer listed, but the little post office and government wharf continued to be a stop for the Union Steamship boats, which the Bells used to ship their cattle to area logging camps. The wharf was also the site of a short-lived alder mill. In 1937, the population registered at the Bold Point post office was 45, but by the 1950s, when boat service stopped, it had dropped to 29.

Moses Ireland's death was not the last to provoke controversy at Bold Point. A rancher named Captain G.T. Dunn, a veteran of the Riel Rebellion, set out in his small boat in December 1936 to pick up, among other things, a cabbage. When his body was found slung overboard and bound in ropes, residents concluded there had been foul play. The cabbage he sought was sitting on his kitchen table along with the remains of a couple of whiskey glasses, suggesting that Dunn had made it home before his boating accident. Dunn was an unpopular fellow, who took in a mail-order bride, later admitting he had a family elsewhere; and in 1932 he paid a fine of $25 and spent one day in jail for shooting a neighbour's horse. While Bold Point people still contended years later that Dunn had been murdered, the Campbell River police concluded it was an accident, resulting from tying his sail lines to his leg.[19]

Another untimely death that smacks of folklore was that of an unnamed accident victim

A young lad in chaps at Bell's Ranch, Bold Point, c. 1935. The dog may be one of three pets that have been immortalized with a marble headstone and wrought iron fence. **MCR 6754 Woolsey Collection.**

who was buried on Bold Island. When the man's dog persisted in howling over his grave, residents decided to dig the man up. Scrapings on the lid of the coffin indicated he had been alive when they buried him, but by the time the man was exhumed he was well and truly dead.

The only grave visible today at Bold Point is at the crest of the hill leading down to the dock. A beloved horse and several dogs belonging to the Bell family have a headstone, while Moses Ireland's daughter-in-law, Lilly Ward, and another person, lay in an unmarked grave a stone's throw to the east.

In the 1970s and '80s, Village Bay Lakes and Bold Point drew an influx of newcomers, back-to-the-landers taking up subdivided portions of the original settlers' ranches. About 30 people continue to live in the area year around, some of them boating their children across to nearby Read Island to attend school.

Mount Seymour Trail

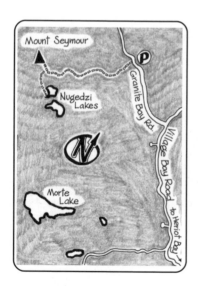

How to Get There: Drive 2 kilometres (1.2 miles) along Granite Bay Road and park on the right hand side. There is a 450-metre (1,462-foot) elevation gain in 3.7 kilometres (2.2 miles) so it is best to allow 5 hours to reach the summit and return. Note: If you have a second vehicle, leave one at the Nugedzi Trail head and drive to the Mount Seymour Trail. A connecting trail just past the sign for the summit

84

allows a round trip along both trails. This is a full day hike—one of the best on Quadra.

This hike goes up to the highest point on Quadra Island and yields spectacular views of the Coast Mountains, old-growth by Nugedzi Lake, and mountains on Vancouver Island. The trail stays on the west/south side of the summit, making it a sunny hike once you are clear of the forest.

Start off following an old logging road bounded by Sword Fern, Salal, and Deer Fern through second-growth Douglas-fir, Western Hemlock, and Western Redcedar. Near the marsh you can see Labrador Tea, Swamp Gentian, Skunk Cabbage, and if you're lucky, a Rough-skinned Newt. In May in the mixed old growth, you can find up to six species of orchid: Fairyslipper, Western Coralroot, Heart-leaved, Northwest and Broad-leaved Twayblade, and Rattlesnake Plantain. You also might see Indian-pipe, Single Delight, White-veined Wintergreen, Lyall's Anemone,

View toward Read and Cortes Islands

and Davidson's Penstemon. Near the edge of the forest is a signpost to the summit, with rock cairns to follow, and just beyond is a sign for the connector trail to Nugedzi Lake.

As you head up to the summit, pay close attention to the next cairn: it is easy to wander off the trail while you are enjoying wonderful views over Nugedzi and Little Nugedzi Lake. In the summer, Band-tailed Pigeons, Nighthawks and Turkey Vultures frequent the summit. In the winter, you can find Gray Jays and Blue Grouse amongst the Crowberry, White Pine and Juniper.

Lucky Jim Mine

How to Get There: The fun of discovering crumbling log cabins, a giant iron wheel, and mine shafts hidden in second-growth forest near Granite Bay make Lucky Jim Mine one of the most intriguing heritage sites on the island. The mine is approximately 6 kilometres (4 miles) from the Granite Bay/ Village Bay Road intersection, on a well-maintained gravel road. The first sign of it, which requires careful spotting, is a slumped log cabin at the right hand side of the road, where a side road intersects the main road.

Loggers working for the BC Mills Timber and Trading Company (the Hastings outfit) are said to have discovered the ore body in their workings in about 1903. Principals of

The Luoma family, Finnish settlers at Granite Bay, were hired to build cabins for the labourers at Lucky Jim Mine, in about 1910. The fallen timbers of these split-log structures can still be seen along the old railway grade near the abandoned mine. Photographer: Henry Twidle. **MCR 5108, Adams Collection**

the logging company formed a subsidiary, the Great Granite Development Syndicate Company, in 1907 and hauled ore using the company train.

By 1910, the mine was at its peak. Log and slab miners' bunkhouses were built along either side of the railway's mainline and 1,092 metric tonnes (1,200 tons) of copper, gold, and silver-bearing ore were shipped monthly. The main shaft was down to 34 metres (110 feet), with the higher grade ore present at the 23-metre (75-foot) level. Although only the first few shipments are said to have been profitable, the mine remained in production until a massive forest fire in 1925 wiped it out, narrowly missing the miners' shacks.

Several mining companies have continued to hold options on Lucky Jim over the years, including Butler Mountain, which did exploratory work there in the 1980s. But after several months of work and much expense, refurbishing the mine shafts and testing the ore, the company decided not to proceed. The ore was apparently not

"Old Curly," seen here at Granite Bay in 1911, may have been the first train used for logging in BC. The train is now on exhibit at the Burnaby Heritage Village. **Photographer: Henry Twidle. MCR 6012, Adams Collection.**

valuable enough to warrant the expense of extraction. The company capped off the two main shafts, but these boards are now in disrepair, requiring caution on the part of visitors to the old mine.

Part of the reason Lucky Jim was expensive to mine was water seepage. A giant iron wheel, hauled to the mine sometime prior to 1925, was used to pump water out of the mine. Adding to the jumble of mine refuse, residents of the area have dropped off an iron furnace from a nearby homestead and a small steam donkey used for hauling logs. The giant iron wheel, the ruins of the miners' bunkhouses, and samples of crumbling copper and fool's gold give this place continuing appeal.

Newton Lake Trail

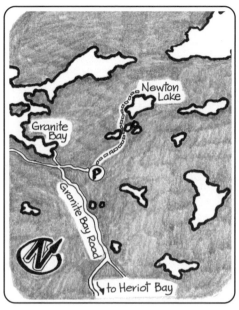

How to Get There: On the Granite Bay Road just before reaching the ocean, turn after crossing a bridge, onto a small logging road, then continue 300 metres (0.2 miles). Watch for the trail sign on your left and a small parking area. This is a moderate hike for 3.24 kilometres (1.9 miles) that should take about 2-4 hours.

The trail follows a former logging road past some small lakes to Newton Lake. By the small lakes in the spring there is Hardhack, Sweet Gale, Labrador Tea, Skunk Cabbage, Round-leafed Sundew, Swamp Gentian, and occasionally evidence of beaver activity. An Osprey pair also nests at the far end of the last small lake. Newton Lake has excellent swimming from a south-facing rocky headland and is surrounded by second-growth Hemlock

Podlike follicles remain on the stems of Hardhack shrubs after the leaves have fallen.

89

and Douglas-fir. Wolf and cougar scat is often found on the trail. A connecting trail leads down to Small Inlet and Waiatt Bay.

Granite Bay

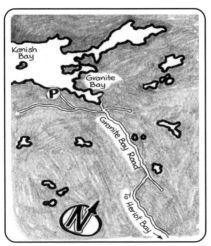

How to Get There: The interconnected inlets of Kanish Bay and Granite Bay on the north end of Quadra Island provided a safe haven for First Nations groups who wintered there in times past. Some of the most extensive archaeological sites in the district can be found on this part of Quadra Island, accessible by boat from the fish farm dock at the end of the Granite Bay Road. There is also evidence in the bay of its history as one of the largest railway logging camps in the region, starting in the 1890s. To reach the fish farm dock take the left turn after a bridge, just before you reach the end of the road at Granite Bay. This dirt road, which is in poor condition, forks to the right, leading to a boat launch. Be prepared for a slimy beach at low tide!

Paddling through Granite Bay, Kanish Bay, and Small Inlet by kayak or canoe makes an excellent day trip. Just outside Granite Bay is Shell Island, a little tidal island where the white clamshell beach denotes thousands of years of use by the First Nations people. Every inch of the island, from its rocky promontory looking out into Discovery Passage, to the south-facing benchland with its curving beach, is covered with midden. At low tide it's possible to see a V-shaped stone fish trap between Shell Island and

Quadra Island. This stone base once supported a weir used to ensnare fish at the changing of the tide.

Beyond Shell Island is a massive archaeological site at Orchard Bay, just to the north of the entrance to Small Inlet. In times past, this was a major village site, perhaps a point of congregation for various tribes during winter. In the early twentieth century, a man named McIntyre built a homestead atop the rich soil of the old midden. His mature orchard still bears an abundance of fruit.

At the end of Small Inlet, a hiking trail crosses Quadra Island at its narrowest point, a walk of about 60 minutes return, leading to yet another extensive clamshell midden at Waiatt Bay. This was a place where several Lekwiltok tribes stayed for a period of time, in the days when the group was moving southward, prior to taking over Discovery Passage. The Lekwiltok appear to have made little use of the old village sites in Kanish and Granite Bay, except for seasonal food gathering. It's likely the original

Granite Bay, c. 1916. There were two stores and a rudimentary hotel at Granite Bay when the "Hastings outfit" (BC Mills Timber and Trading Company) logged by rail at the bay, from about 1890 to 1925. Photographer: Henry Twidle. **MCR 7843, Adams Collection.**

inhabitants were a Coast Salish group, the Island Comox, who once dominated the region.

In the nineteenth century, Granite Bay served as a base for one of the largest logging operations in the district. The Hastings Company (BC Mills Timber and Trading Company of Vancouver) pioneered railway logging in BC at their Granite Bay operation, using an old steam engine retired from CPR construction. "Old Curly," as the engine was nicknamed, is now on display at the Burnaby Heritage Village

At the peak of operations in the 1890s, the Hastings outfit employed up to 200 men. A little settlement sprang up around their beach camp and log dump, including a store/post office, school, hotel, brothel, and a government dock where the Union Steamship called to deliver passengers, mail, and supplies. About six ranches were established along the company's mainline, many of them pre-empted by Finnish settlers.

When the Union Steamship discontinued its service to little communities like Granite Bay in the early 1950s, the population dropped and it was no longer feasible for schools, stores, and other services to operate there. Granite Bay c. 1930. Photographer: Henry Twidle. **MCR 4184**

Campbell River pioneer, Fred Nunns, wrote a diary account of his epic journey in 1890 to take produce to a camp in Granite Bay:

Wednesday Oct. 22: Fine. I left with a canoe load of pumpkins and squash for Grant's camp at Granite Point... Was late on the tide and when I got to Seymour Narrows found the tide was rushing through Canoe Pass like a mill race so camped and slept there.

Thursday Oct. 23: This morning 2 a.m. I got up to put fresh logs on fire then went to look at canoe. Found tide in going out had left her on a rock and she had capsized and the pumpkins and squash were floating all around. Lit a fire near canoe and collected them. Found I had lost 9 pumpkins and 24 squash. Got through Narrows at daybreak and had a hard pull up to Grant's where I arrived 11 a.m. wet through, as it had been raining all morning. Found Grant was not there but expected in afternoon. ... Sundown the 'Rainbow' came in and the men got a lot of liquor and had a regular drunken night of it. I never got a wink of sleep.

Friday October 24: Cloudy and threatening. S.S. 'Thistle' came in 8 a.m. Sold my pumpkins at 37 cents each and squash at 12 cents to Grant. Bought 5 bags of crushed barley for my hogs, 1 box cartridges, 3 large bot. of sauce and got about 20 books. Started home 10:30 a.m.

Where there was a logging camp there was usually a "house of ill-repute," often company-sanctioned, as a way of attracting and keeping men in camp. Granite Bay was no exception. The Columbia Coast Mission, a marine-based arm of the Anglican Church, chose Granite Bay for their first attempt at stopping the logging camp sex trade. Missionary John Antle reported that the men initially held an indignation meeting to try to stop the preacher, but the church prevailed. With the support of the camp foreman, who claimed the women distracted his men from their work, the ladies of the night were routed from the camp.

No road connected north and south Quadra Island until 1951, making them entirely separate communities. Granite Bay folk had to walk a rough trail to attend dances and social functions at the south end of the island. Irene Stramberg knitted as she made the long trek. In 1903, Frederick Yeatman wrote to his wife on south Quadra Island from the logging camp at Granite Bay, sending his letter by a passing freight boat:

> [I] have been working on the boom the last week and riding up and down on the train, the camp is two miles in from the beach. I don't know as I will be able to send my washing home. I have plenty of clean clothes to last quite a while, but if I see anyone coming that way I may send some; if not I might wash a little. I don't suppose I shall be able to come home until I come for good, unless I walk home. I may possibly do that but it is a pretty good walk. If you are sending some papers you can send a map of the island. I think there is a broken piece with the island on it. And send the compass too.

With the passing years, the Hastings outfit was replaced by small truck-logging operations, running along the old railway grades and trestles. The little community at Granite Bay expanded and contracted with changing log prices, sometimes including a cluster of rudimentary float houses tied up in the bay.

In 1953, Union Steamship service was discontinued, spelling the end of the community, even though a public road was pushed through to south Quadra in 1951. Within a few years the store and school at the bay closed. Today fewer than 50 people live in the vicinity of Granite Bay, among whom is Al Luoma, a descendant of one of the original Finnish settlers.

Place Names: *Kanish Bay* would be more accurately pronounced in English as KAH-neese Bay, according to George Quocksister, a Lekwala speaker who translates the meaning to "you can walk through to the other side." *Waiatt Bay* was said by Lekwala speaker, James Smith, to mean "that which has a river." Yet another First Nations informant, Peter Wilson, said a more accurate English pronunciation would be Wuad, meaning "place that has herring" or "place where herring spawn" (Isenor, Stephens, Watson 1989: 93). *Orchard Bay* is a local name, not officially designated, describing the abundant orchard planted there in about 1900.

End Notes

[1]. The oldest archaeological site in the north Vancouver Island region is at Bear Cove, near Port Hardy, which has been dated at 8,000 years before the present. On Quadra Island a skull found by chance at the current village of the We-Wai-Kai people, at Cape Mudge, was dated at 2,000 years old.

[2]. Edward Curtis, *The North American Indian*, Volume 10 (New York: Johnson Reprint Corporation, 1978) p. 111.

[3]. Homer Barnett, *The Coast Salish of British Columbia* (Eugene OR: University of Oregon Press, 1955), p. 25.

[4]. Barnett, *The Coast Salish*, p. 167.

[5]. Robert Galois, *Kwakwaka'wakw Settlements, 1775-1920, A Geographical Analysis and Gazetteer* (Vancouver: UBC Press, 1994), p. 38, Table 1.3.

[6]. Letter to the Editor, Nanaimo Free Press, August 19, 1890.

[7]. Galois, *Kwakwaka'wakw Settlements*, p. 275.

[8]. Mrs. Ward, *Log of the Columbia*, 1906, BC Archives & Records Services.

[9]. Anna Joyce, unpublished memoirs, Museum at Campbell River Archives.

[10]. Comox Argus newspaper, January 3, 1924.

[11]. Fred Nunns's diary, BC Archives and Records Services.

[12]. Wilson and Brady went bankrupt shortly after this and were taken over by Abbott Timber.

[13]. George Pidcock's diary, BC Archives and Records Services.

[14]. Galois, *Kwakwaka'wakw Settlements*, p. 274.

[15]. Harry Assu with Joy Inglis, *Assu of Cape Mudge: Recollections of a Coastal Indian Chief* (Vancouver: UBC Press, 1989), pp. 57, 99.

[16]. *Log of the Columbia*, July 1906, Volume I, Number 5, BC Archives & Records Services.

[17]. The first mention of H.A. Bull on Quadra Island, that has been found to date, is in the November issue of the Weekly-News Advertiser of Vancouver, in November 1895. In the January 10, 1896 issue Bull's name is connected with a hotel and store in Heriot Bay. The *Comox* stopped there weekly to drop mail and supplies for the store. Bull may have taken over the Hotel Dallas, owned by the island's first non-Native settler Charles Dallas. Little is known of Hotel Dallas except that it was in the vicinity of Heriot Bay, which was originally called Dallasville. The first dance on the island was held at Hotel Dallas on October 12, 1895, as reported in the Weekly-News Advertiser.

[18]. Memory of Donnie Haas, as told to Richard Mackie, June 1999.

[19]. Comox Argus newspaper, July 25, 1932 and January 21, 1937, Museum at Campbell River Archives.

Selected Bibliography

Andersen, Doris. *Evergreen Islands, The Islands of the Inside Passage: Quadra to Malcolm.* Sidney: Gray's Publishing, 1979.

Assu, Harry, with Inglis, Joy. *Assu of Cape Mudge, Recollections of a Coastal Indian Chief.* Vancouver: UBC Press, 1989.

Cannings, Richard and Sydney. *British Columbia: A Natural History* Vancouver Greystone Press, 1996

Grady, Wayne. *Vultures: Nature's Ghastly Gourmet* Vancouver Greystone Press 1997

Inglis, Joy. *Spirit in the Stone.* Victoria: Horsdal & Schubart, 1998.

Ludvigsen, Rolf and Graham Beard *West Coast Fossils: A Guide to Ancient Life of Vancouver Island* Vancouver, Whitecap 1994

Stewart, Hilary. *Artifacts of the Northwest Coast Indians.* North Vancouver: Hancock House Publishers, 1981.

Stewart, Hilary. *Cedar, Tree of Life to the Northwest Coast Indians.* Vancouver: Douglas and McIntyre, 1984.

Stewart, Hilary. *On Island Time.* Vancouver: Douglas and McIntyre, 1998.

Taylor, Jeanette. *River City, A History of Campbell River and the Discovery Islands.* Madeira Park, BC: Harbour Publishing, 1999.

Index